CHEAP EATS

CHEAP EATS

COLLINS & BROWN

The Good Housekeeping website is
www.goodhousekeeping.co.uk

ISBN 978-1-908449-96-2

A catalogue record for this book is available from
the British Library.

Reproduction by Dot Gradations Ltd, UK
Printed and bound by
1010 Printing International Ltd, China

This book can be ordered direct from the publisher.
Contact the marketing department, but try your
bookshop first.

www.anovabooks.com

NOTES

Both metric and imperial measures are given for
the recipes. Follow either set of measures, not a
mixture of both, as they are not interchangeable.

All spoon measures are level.
1 tsp = 5ml spoon; 1 tbsp = 15ml spoon.

Ovens and grills must be preheated to the specified
temperature.

Medium eggs should be used except where
otherwise specified. Free-range eggs are
recommended.

Note that some recipes contain raw or lightly
cooked eggs. The young, elderly, pregnant women
and anyone with an immune-deficiency disease
should avoid these because of the slight risk
of salmonella.

Contents

Bites and Sides
for Loose Change

Keep it Seasonal

Why? Because not only will the produce you buy taste fantastic, it will also cost less. Look out for good deals at supermarkets, farm shops, markets and greengrocers, where you can sometimes buy larger, cheaper quantities for freezing or batch cooking. Pick Your Own farms often charge half the price of the supermarkets. You can pick fruit and vegetables at their ripest and enjoy a fun day out with the family too.

January

Vegetables Beetroot, Brussels sprouts, cauliflower, celeriac, celery, chicory, Jerusalem artichokes, kale, leeks, parsnips, potatoes (maincrop), rhubarb, swede, turnips

Fruit Apples, clementines, kiwi fruit, lemons, oranges, passion fruit, pears, pineapple, pomegranate, satsumas, tangerines, walnuts

Fish Clams, cockles, haddock, hake, lemon sole, mussels, plaice

February

Vegetables Brussels sprouts, cauliflower, celeriac, chicory, kale, leeks, parsnips, potatoes (maincrop), rhubarb, swede

Fruit Bananas, blood oranges, kiwi fruit, lemons, oranges, passion fruit, pears, pineapple, pomegranate

Fish Cockles, cod, haddock, hake, lemon sole, mussels, salmon

March

Vegetables Cauliflower, chicory, kale, leeks, purple sprouting broccoli, rhubarb, spring onions

Fruit Bananas, blood oranges, kiwi fruit, lemons, oranges, passion fruit, pineapple, pomegranate

Fish Cockles, cod, hake, lemon sole, mussels, salmon, sea trout

April

Vegetables Asparagus, broccoli, Jersey royal potatoes, purple sprouting broccoli, radishes, rhubarb, rocket, spinach, spring onions, watercress

Fruit Bananas, kiwi fruit

Fish Cockles, cod, salmon, sea trout

May

Vegetables Asparagus, broccoli, Jersey royal potatoes, new potatoes, radishes, rhubarb, rocket, spinach, spring onions, watercress

Fruit Cherries, kiwi fruit, strawberries

Meat Lamb

Fish Cod, crab, lemon sole, plaice, salmon, sea bass, sea trout

June

Vegetables Artichokes, asparagus, aubergines, broad beans, broccoli, carrots, courgettes, fennel, mangetouts, Jersey royal potatoes, new potatoes, peas, radishes, rocket, runner beans, spring onions, turnips, watercress

Fruit Cherries, strawberries

Meat Lamb

Fish Cod, crab, haddock, herring, lemon sole, mackerel, plaice, salmon, sardines, sea bass, sea trout

July

Vegetables Artichokes, aubergines, beetroot, broad beans, broccoli, carrots, courgettes, cucumber, fennel, French beans, garlic, mangetouts, new potatoes, onions, peas, potatoes (maincrop), radishes, rocket, runner beans, turnips, watercress

Fruit Apricots, blackberries, blueberries, cherries, gooseberries, greengages, kiwi fruit, melons, peaches, raspberries, redcurrants, strawberries, tomatoes

Meat Lamb, rabbit

Fish Cod, crab, haddock, herring, lemon sole, mackerel, plaice, salmon, sardines, sea bass, sea trout

August

Vegetables Artichokes, aubergines, beetroot, broad beans, broccoli, carrots, courgettes, cucumber, fennel, French beans, garlic, leeks, mangetouts, marrow, new potatoes, onions, peas, peppers, potatoes (maincrop), radishes, rocket, runner beans, sweetcorn, watercress

Fruit Apricots, blackberries, blueberries, damsons, greengages, kiwi fruit, melons, nectarines, peaches, plums, raspberries, redcurrants, tomatoes

Meat Lamb, rabbit

Fish Cod, crab, grey mullet, haddock, herring, lemon sole, mackerel, plaice, salmon, sardines, sea bass

September

Vegetables Artichokes, aubergines, beetroot, broccoli, butternut squash, carrots, courgettes, cucumber, fennel, garlic, leeks, mangetouts, marrow, onions, parsnips, peas, peppers, potatoes (maincrop), radishes, rocket, runner beans, sweetcorn, watercress, wild mushrooms

Fruit Apples, blackberries, damsons, figs, grapes, melons, nectarines, peaches, pears, plums, raspberries, redcurrants, tomatoes, walnuts

Meat Lamb, rabbit

Fish Clams, cod, crab, grey mullet, haddock, herring, lemon sole, mackerel, plaice, sea bass, squid

October

Vegetables Artichokes, beetroot, broccoli, butternut squash, carrots, celeriac, celery, fennel, kale, leeks, marrow, onions, parsnips, potatoes (maincrop), pumpkin, swede, turnips, watercress, wild mushrooms
Fruit Apples, chestnuts, figs, pears, quince, tomatoes, walnuts
Meat Rabbit
Fish Brill, clams, crab, grey mullet, haddock, hake, lemon sole, mackerel, mussels, plaice, sea bass, squid

November

Vegetables Artichokes, beetroot, Brussels sprouts, celeriac, celery, chicory, kale, leeks, parsnips, potatoes (maincrop), pumpkin, swede, turnips, watercress, wild mushrooms
Fruit Apples, chestnuts, clementines, cranberries, figs, passion fruit, pears, quince, satsumas, tangerines, walnuts
Meat Rabbit
Fish Brill, clams, haddock, hake, lemon sole, mussels, plaice, sea bass, squid

December

Vegetables Beetroot, Brussels sprouts, cauliflower, celeriac, celery, chicory, kale, leeks, parsnips, potatoes (maincrop), pumpkin, swede, turnips
Fruit Apples, chestnuts, clementines, cranberries, passion fruit, pears, pineapple, pomegranate, satsumas, tangerines, walnuts
Meat Rabbit
Fish Brill, clams, haddock, hake, lemon sole, mussels, plaice, sea bass

Spanish Omelette

Hands-on time: 15 minutes
Cooking time: about 35 minutes

900g (2lb) potatoes, peeled and
  left whole

3–4 tbsp vegetable oil

1 onion, finely sliced

8 medium eggs

3 tbsp freshly chopped flat-leafed parsley

3 streaky bacon rashers

salt and freshly ground black pepper

green salad to serve

1 Add the potatoes to a pan of cold
   salted water and bring to the boil, then
   reduce the heat and simmer for 15–20
   minutes until almost cooked. Drain
   and leave until cool enough to handle,
   then slice thickly.

2 Meanwhile, preheat the grill. Heat
   1 tbsp of the oil in an 18cm (7in)
   non-stick frying pan (suitable for use
   under the grill). Add the onion and fry
   gently for 7–10 minutes until softened.
   Take off the heat and put to one side.

3 Lightly beat the eggs in a bowl and
   season well with salt and ground
   black pepper.

4 Heat the remaining oil in the frying
   pan, then layer the potato slices,
   onion and 2 tbsp of the chopped
   parsley in the pan. Pour in the beaten
   eggs and cook for 5–10 minutes until
   the omelette is firm underneath.
   Meanwhile, grill the bacon until golden
   and crisp, then break into pieces.

5 Put the omelette in its pan under
   the grill for 2–3 minutes until the
   top is just set. Scatter the bacon and
   remaining chopped parsley over the
   surface. Serve cut into wedges, with a
   green salad.

Serves 4

Welsh Rarebit

Hands-on time: 10 minutes
Cooking time: about 15 minutes

400g can chopped tomatoes

½ tbsp tomato purée

1 small shallot, finely sliced

175g (6oz) Caerphilly or mature
   Cheddar, grated

½ tsp English mustard

50ml (2fl oz) ale

a few dashes of Worcestershire sauce

1 large egg yolk

1½ tbsp finely chopped fresh parsley

8 crumpets

salt and freshly ground black pepper

crisp green salad to serve

1 Put the tomatoes, tomato purée and
   shallot into a small pan. Bring to the
   boil, then reduce the heat and simmer
   for 10 minutes. Check the seasoning.

2 Meanwhile, mix the cheese, mustard,
   ale, Worcestershire sauce, egg yolk,
   parsley and seasoning to taste
   together in a bowl.

3 Preheat the grill to medium. Arrange
   the crumpets on a baking sheet and
   toast until golden. Divide and spread
   the tomato sauce equally over the
   toasted crumpets, then top each
   with an equal amount of the cheese
   mixture. Grill for 3–5 minutes until
   bubbling and golden. Serve with a
   crisp green salad.

SAVE TIME

Make the tomato sauce mixture
up to a day ahead. Cool, cover and
chill. When ready to serve, reheat
gently and complete the recipe.

Serves 4

Make Your Own Soup

Soups are nutritious, full of flavour and easy to make. Incredibly versatile, they can be smooth or chunky, light for a first course or substantial for a main course, made with vegetables, pulses, meat, chicken or fish.

You can use almost any mixture of vegetables.

To serve four, you will need:
1 or 2 finely chopped onions, 2 tbsp oil or 1 tbsp oil and 25g (1oz) butter, 1 or 2 crushed garlic cloves (optional), 450g (1lb) chopped mixed vegetables, such as leeks, potatoes, celery, fennel, canned tomatoes and parsnips (finely chopped or cut into larger dice for a chunky soup), 1.1 litres (2 pints) stock.

1 Fry the onions in the oil or oil and butter until soft and add the garlic, if you like.
2 Add the chopped mixed vegetables and the stock. Bring to the boil, then reduce the heat and simmer for 20–30 minutes until the vegetables are tender.
3 Leave chunky, partially purée or blend until smooth.

Puréeing soups

1 **Using a jug blender** Allow the soup to cool slightly, then fill the jug about half-full, making sure that there is more liquid than solids. Cover the lid with a teatowel and hold it on tightly. Blend until smooth, then add more solids and blend again until all the soup is smooth. (If you have a lot of soup, transfer each batch to a clean pan.)

1

2 **Using a stick blender** Allow the soup to cool slightly. Stick the blender deep into the soup, switch it on and move it about so that all the soup is puréed.

Note: don't do this in a non-stick pan.

3 **Using a mouli** A mouli-légumes makes a fine purée, although it takes longer than using a blender. Fit the fine plate to the mouli-légumes and set it over a bowl – put a teatowel underneath to keep it from moving on the table. Fill the bowl of the mouli about halfway up the sides, putting in more solids than liquid. Work in batches if you have a large quantity of soup.

4 **Using a sieve** If you don't have a blender or mouli-légumes, you can purée soup by pushing it through a sieve, although this will take a much longer time.

Partially puréed soups

1 For an interesting texture, purée one-third to half of the ingredients, then stir back into the soup.

2 Alternatively, prepare the vegetables or other ingredients, but keep a few choice pieces to one side. While the soup is cooking, steam or boil these pieces until just tender; refresh green vegetables in cold water. Just before serving, cut into smaller pieces and add to the soup.

Chunky soups

1 Cut the ingredients into bite-size pieces. Heat oil or butter in the soup pan and cook the onions – and garlic if you like – until soft and lightly coloured.

2 Add the remaining ingredients, putting in those that need the longest cooking first. Pour in some stock and bring to the boil.

3 Reduce the heat and simmer gently until all the ingredients are tender. If too much liquid boils away, just add more.

Scotch Broth

Hands-on time: 15 minutes
Cooking time: about 1 hour

1 tbsp vegetable oil

250g (9oz) lamb neck fillets, cut into 2cm (¾in) cubes

2 parsnips, roughly chopped

2 carrots, roughly chopped

1 onion, finely chopped

1 potato, finely diced

3 smoked streaky bacon rashers, finely sliced

125g (4oz) pearl barley

1 litre (1¾ pints) lamb stock

75g (3oz) frozen peas

salt and freshly ground black pepper

a small handful of fresh parsley, finely chopped, to garnish

1 Heat the oil over a high heat in a large casserole. Brown the lamb all over – do this in batches if necessary to stop the lamb from sweating rather than browning. Add the parsnips, carrots, onion, potato and bacon and fry for 3–5 minutes.

2 Add the pearl barley and mix well. Pour in the stock and stir well, scraping any sticky goodness from the bottom of the casserole. Bring to the boil, then reduce the heat, cover and simmer gently for 40–50 minutes until the lamb is tender.

3 Stir in the peas, heat through, then check the seasoning. Transfer to individual bowls, garnish the broth with parsley and serve.

SAVE MONEY

Neck is an ideal cut of lamb to use if you are watching your wallet, and pearl barley adds great texture and body.

Serves 4

Spiced Cauliflower Soup

Hands-on time: 15 minutes
Cooking time: 35 minutes

1 tbsp chilli oil, plus extra to drizzle

1 medium onion, chopped

1 garlic clove, crushed

2 tsp ground coriander

1 medium cauliflower, cut into florets

1 large potato, peeled and cubed

1 lemon

1.4 litres (2½ pints) hot chicken stock

2 tsp extra virgin olive oil

6 tsp natural yogurt

salt and freshly ground black pepper

25g (1oz) flaked almonds, toasted,
   to garnish

SAVE TIME

Prepare the soup to the end of step
2. Chill for up to two days. Complete
the recipe to serve.

1 Heat the chilli oil in a large pan and gently fry the onion for 10 minutes or until softened. Add a little salt to the pan now – it gives extra depth of flavour to the soup. Add the garlic and coriander and fry for 2 minutes. Stir in the cauliflower and potato and cook for 3 minutes.

2 Zest the lemon and add the zest to the pan with the hot stock. Season and bring to the boil, then reduce the heat, cover and simmer for 15–20 minutes until the vegetables are tender. Cool slightly. Whiz the soup in batches until smooth.

3 Pour the soup back into the rinsed-out pan. Reheat gently and check the seasoning. Divide among six warmed bowls.

4 Juice half the lemon and mix with the olive oil. Swirl 1 tsp yogurt into each bowl. Drizzle with the lemon oil and some extra chilli oil, if you like, then garnish with the almonds. Serve immediately.

The Well-stocked Fridge and Freezer

Having the right equipment can make life so much easier in the kitchen. Consider the space you have available: do you have room for a separate fridge and freezer? Choose wisely to ensure you get the most out of what you can fit in your kitchen.

The perfect fridge

The fridge is vital for any kitchen and keeps food fresh for longer. However, it is the main culprit for waste. The bigger it is, the more it becomes a repository for out-of-date condiments and bags of wilted salad leaves that lurk in its depths.

Safe storage

- ❑ Cool cooked food to room temperature before putting in the fridge
- ❑ Wrap or cover all food except fruit and vegetables

- ❑ Practise fridge discipline: the coldest shelves are at the bottom so store raw meat, fish and poultry there
- ❑ Separate cooked foods from raw foods

To make sure the fridge works properly:

- ❑ Don't overfill it
- ❑ Don't put hot foods in it
- ❑ Don't open the door more than necessary
- ❑ Clean it regularly

The perfect freezer

This is an invaluable storage tool and if you use it properly – particularly with batch cooking – you can save time and avoid wastage. Make sure you allow the food time to thaw: if you leave it overnight in the fridge, your meal will be ready to pop into the oven when you get home from work. You can have all sorts of standbys waiting for you: breads, cakes, pastry, frozen vegetables, fruit such as raspberries and blackberries, and cream, stocks, soups, herbs and bacon.

How to store food:
- ❏ Freeze food as soon as possible after purchase
- ❏ Label cooked food with the date and name of the dish
- ❏ Freeze food in portions
- ❏ Never put warm foods into the freezer; wait until they have cooled
- ❏ Check the manufacturer's instructions for freezing times
- ❏ Do not refreeze food once it has thawed

What not to store in the freezer:
- ❏ Whole eggs – freeze whites and yolks separately
- ❏ Fried foods – they lose their crispness and can go soggy
- ❏ Vegetables – cucumber, lettuce and celery have too high a water content
- ❏ Some sauces – mayonnaise and similar sauces will separate when thawed

To make sure the freezer works properly:
- ❏ Defrost it regularly
- ❏ Keep the freezer as full as possible

Thawing and reheating food:
Each recipe will give you instructions, but generally:
- ❏ Some foods, such as vegetables, soups and sauces, can be cooked from frozen – dropped into boiling water, or heated until thawed
- ❏ Ensure other foods are thoroughly thawed before cooking
- ❏ Cook food as soon as possible after thawing
- ❏ Ensure food is piping hot all the way through after cooking

Anchovy Pizza-tart

Hands-on time: 20 minutes, plus rising
Cooking time: about 40 minutes

200g (7oz) strong white flour, plus extra
  to dust

½ tsp fast-action dried yeast

½ tsp caster sugar

¼ tsp salt

2 large onions, finely sliced

125ml (4fl oz) vegetable oil

12 anchovies, marinated in oil, halved
  lengthways

15 cherry tomatoes, halved

1 tbsp chopped fresh chives

green salad to serve

1 Sift the flour into a large bowl and mix
  in the yeast, sugar and salt. Quickly stir
  in 150ml (¼ pint) tepid water to make
  a soft but not sticky dough. Tip on to a
  lightly floured worksurface and knead
  for 3 minutes. Put back into the bowl,
  cover with clingfilm and leave to rise
  in a warm place for 20 minutes.

2 Meanwhile, put the onions into a
  pan and pour the oil over them. Fry
  gently for 15 minutes until soft. Strain,
  keeping the oil to one side.

3 Preheat the oven to 200°C (180°C
  fan oven) mark 6. Lightly dust a
  worksurface with flour and roll out
  the dough into a 30 × 30cm (12 × 12in)
  square. Transfer to a non-stick baking
  sheet. Brush with some of the reserved
  onion oil, then spread the onions
  over. Use the anchovy strips to make
  a diagonal crisscross pattern on top
  of the onions. Put a tomato half, cut
  side up, in the centre of each diamond.
  Cook in the oven for 20–25 minutes
  until golden. Scatter with chives and
  serve in slices with a green salad.

Serves 4

Iberian Potatoes

Hands-on time: 15 minutes
Cooking time: about 1½ hours

2 tbsp olive oil

2 medium onions, thinly sliced

2 garlic cloves, slivered

3 medium baking potatoes, thinly sliced

4 tomatoes, sliced

1 tsp dried oregano

500ml (17fl oz) vegetable stock

salt and freshly ground black pepper

1 Preheat the oven to 200°C (180°C fan oven) mark 6. Heat the oil in a large flameproof casserole dish and gently fry the onions for 10 minutes or until softened. Add the garlic and cook for 1 minute. Take the casserole off the heat and use a slotted spoon to lift out the onion mixture and put to one side.

2 Put half the potato slices into the bottom of the casserole dish, then layer on the onion mixture followed by the tomato slices. Sprinkle with the oregano and lots of seasoning. Finish with a layer of the remaining potato slices, then pour the stock over.

3 Cover and cook in the oven for 1¼ hours, removing the lid for the final 30–40 minutes of cooking time to allow the potatoes to brown. Serve as a side dish.

Serves 4

Braised Red Cabbage and Beetroot

Hands-on time: 15 minutes
Cooking time: about 2¼ hours

1 tbsp olive oil

1 medium onion, finely chopped

1 garlic clove, crushed

2 tbsp dark brown sugar

1 medium red cabbage, shredded

1 medium beetroot, peeled and cut into chunks

leaves from a large fresh thyme sprig

2 tbsp balsamic vinegar

1 tbsp freshly chopped curly parsley

1 Preheat the oven to 170°C (150°C fan oven) mark 3. Heat the oil in a flameproof casserole and gently fry the onion for 10 minutes or until softened. Add the garlic and sugar and fry for 2 minutes.

2 Stir in the cabbage, beetroot, thyme, vinegar and 100ml (3½fl oz) water. Cover and cook in the oven, stirring occasionally, for 2 hours or until tender. Garnish with parsley to serve.

SAVE TIME

This is one of those recipes that tastes even better if you cook it in advance to give the ingredients time to mingle. Complete the recipe but don't add the parsley garnish. Cool and chill for up to two days. Reheat gently over a low heat until piping hot, garnish and serve.

Serves 6

Take 5 Quick Salad Dressings

Lemon Vinaigrette

To make about 150ml (¼ pint), you will need:

2 tbsp lemon juice, 2 tsp runny honey, 8 tbsp extra virgin olive oil, 3 tbsp freshly chopped mint, 4 tbsp roughly chopped fresh flat-leafed parsley, salt and freshly ground black pepper.

1. Put the lemon juice, honey and salt and ground black pepper to taste into a small bowl and whisk to combine. Gradually whisk in the oil and stir in the herbs.
2. If not using immediately, store in a cool place and whisk briefly before using.

Lemon and Parsley

To make about 100ml (3½fl oz), you will need:

juice of ½ lemon, 6 tbsp extra virgin olive oil, 4 tbsp freshly chopped flat-leafed parsley, salt and freshly ground black pepper.

1. Put the lemon juice, oil and parsley into a medium bowl and whisk to combine. Season to taste with salt and ground black pepper.
2. If not using immediately, store in a cool place and whisk briefly before using.

Mustard

To make about 100ml (3½fl oz), you will need:
1 tbsp wholegrain mustard, juice of ½ lemon, 6 tbsp extra virgin olive oil, salt and freshly ground black pepper.

1 Put the mustard, lemon juice and oil into a small bowl and whisk to combine. Season to taste with salt and ground black pepper.
2 If not using immediately, store in a cool place and whisk briefly before using.

Blue Cheese

To make 100ml (3½fl oz), you will need:
50g (2oz) Roquefort cheese, 2 tbsp low-fat yogurt, 1 tbsp white wine vinegar, 5 tbsp extra virgin olive oil, salt and freshly ground black pepper.

1 Crumble the cheese into a food processor and add the yogurt, vinegar and oil. Whiz for 1 minute until thoroughly combined. Season to taste with salt and ground black pepper.

2 Store in a cool place and use within one day.

Chilli Lime

To make 125ml (4fl oz), you will need:
¼ red chilli, seeded and finely chopped (see Safety Tip, page 34), 1 crushed garlic clove, 1cm (½in) peeled and finely grated piece fresh root ginger, juice of 1½ large limes, 50ml (2fl oz) olive oil, 1½ tbsp light muscovado sugar, 2 tbsp fresh coriander leaves, 2 tbsp fresh mint leaves.

1 Put the chilli, garlic, ginger, lime juice, oil and sugar into a food processor or blender and whiz for 10 seconds to combine.
2 Add the coriander and mint and whiz together for 5 seconds to chop roughly.
3 Store in a cool place and use within two days.

Chicory with Ham and Cheese

TAKE 5

Hands-on time: 5 minutes
Cooking time: about 10 minutes

4 large green chicory heads, halved lengthways

8 slices honey roast ham

8 slices Gouda cheese

15g (½oz) fresh brown breadcrumbs

crusty bread and a green salad to serve

1 Bring a large pan of water to the boil. Add the chicory heads, reduce the heat and simmer for 3–5 minutes until just tender. Drain well.

2 Preheat the grill to medium. Wrap each cooked chicory half in a slice of ham and arrange, cut side down, on a baking sheet. Lay a piece of cheese over each chicory half and top with some of the breadcrumbs. Grill for 3–5 minutes until piping hot and golden. Serve with crusty bread and a green salad.

Serves 4

Warm Smoked Salmon and Cucumber Salad

🍴 **Hands-on time:** 10 minutes
Cooking time: about 5 minutes

½ tbsp vegetable oil

2.5cm (1in) piece fresh root ginger, peeled and finely chopped

1 green chilli, seeded and finely chopped (see Safety Tip)

1 tbsp sesame seeds

6 baby sweetcorn, finely sliced

300g (11oz) straight-to-wok rice noodles

1 cucumber, peeled into ribbons

1 tbsp toasted sesame oil

1 tbsp soy sauce

120g pack smoked salmon trimmings

salt and freshly ground black pepper

a large handful of fresh coriander, finely chopped, to garnish

lime wedges to serve

1 Heat the vegetable oil in a large frying pan or wok. Add the ginger, chilli and sesame seeds and cook for 1 minute. Stir in the sweetcorn and noodles and cook, stirring frequently, for 3 minutes or until the noodles are tender.

2 Add the cucumber, sesame oil, soy sauce and salmon and heat through. Check the seasoning. Garnish with coriander and serve with lime wedges.

SAFETY TIP

Chillies can be quite mild to blisteringly hot, depending on the type of chilli and its ripeness. Taste a small piece first to check it's not too hot for you. Be extremely careful when handling chillies not to touch or rub your eyes with your fingers, or they will sting. Wash knives immediately after handling chillies. As a precaution, use rubber gloves when preparing them, if you like.

Serves 4

Simple Fried Rice

TAKE 5

Hands-on time: 5 minutes
Cooking time: about 20 minutes

150g (5oz) long-grain rice

2 tbsp sesame oil

3 medium eggs, lightly beaten

250g (9oz) frozen petits pois

250g (9oz) cooked peeled prawns

1 Cook the rice in boiling water for about 10 minutes or according to the pack instructions. Drain well.

2 Heat 1 tsp of the sesame oil in a large, non-stick frying pan. Pour in half the beaten eggs and tilt the pan around over the heat for about 1 minute until the egg is set. Tip the omelette on to a warm plate. Repeat with another 1 tsp sesame oil and the remaining beaten egg to make another omelette. Tip on to another warm plate.

3 Add the remaining oil to the pan and stir in the rice and peas. Stir-fry for 2–3 minutes until the peas are cooked. Stir in the prawns.

4 Roll up the omelettes, roughly chop one-third of one, then slice the remainder into strips. Add the chopped omelette to the rice, peas and prawns and cook for 1–2 minutes until heated through. Divide the fried rice among four serving bowls, top with the sliced omelette and serve immediately..

Serves 4

Sardines on Toast

Hands-on time: 5 minutes
Cooking time: about 10 minutes

4 thick slices wholemeal bread

2 large tomatoes, sliced

2 × 120g cans sardines in olive oil, drained

juice of ½ lemon

a small handful of fresh parsley, chopped

1 Preheat the grill. Toast the slices of bread on both sides.

2 Divide the tomato slices and the sardines among the toast slices and squeeze the lemon juice over them, then put back under the grill for 2–3 minutes to heat through. Scatter the parsley over the sardines and serve immediately.

SAVE EFFORT

An easy way to get a brand new dish is to use a 200g can pilchards in tomato sauce instead of the sardines.

Serves 4

Frugal Family Suppers

Midweek Meal Planner

Week 1

Squash Risotto with Hazelnut Butter

Warm Salmon and Potato Salad

Week 2

Quick Creamy Gnocchi

Spicy Baked Eggs

Week 3

Ham, Leek and Mushroom Fusilli

Cheesy Chicken Crispbakes

Week 4

Orange and Ginger Beef Stir-fry

Creamy Cider Chicken

Cherry Tomato and Goat's Cheese Tart

Stuffed Chicken Thighs

Lamb, Lentil and Chilli Soup

Barbecue Minute Steak Sandwiches

Chicken and Squash Gratin

Mustard Lamb Chops

Spicy Pork Meatballs

Bean and Bacon Stew

Beef Pilaf

Crispy-crumbed Cabbage Linguine

Jarlsberg and Sweet Onion Tart

Smoked Haddock and Spinach Frittata

Squash Risotto with Hazelnut Butter

Hands-on time: 20 minutes
Cooking time: about 50 minutes

1 tbsp vegetable oil

500g (1lb 2oz) butternut squash, peeled and cut into 2cm (¾in) cubes

1 onion, finely chopped

1 garlic clove, finely chopped

300g (11oz) risotto rice, such as Arborio or carnaroli

50ml (2fl oz) white wine

1.1 litres (2 pints) hot vegetable stock

25g (1oz) butter

40g (1½oz) blanched hazelnuts, chopped

4 fresh sage leaves, finely sliced

salt and freshly ground black pepper

1 Heat half the oil in a large pan over a medium heat. Fry the squash, tossing occasionally, for 15–20 minutes until tender. Lift the squash out of the pan and put on a plate.

2 Add the remaining oil to the pan and gently fry the onion for 10 minutes or until tender. Stir in the garlic and rice and cook for 2 minutes or until the rice turns translucent. Stir in the wine and let the mixture bubble, stirring frequently, until the liquid has evaporated.

3 Gradually add the hot stock, one ladleful at a time, adding another ladleful only when the previous one has been absorbed. Stir well after each addition. Continue until the rice is nearly cooked – this will take about 15 minutes.

4 Gently stir the cooked squash into the risotto and reheat. Check the seasoning, then cover the pan with a lid and put to one side.

5 Heat the butter and hazelnuts together in a small frying pan until the butter is light brown and the nuts are lightly toasted, then add the sage. Divide the risotto among four warmed bowls, garnish with the hazelnut butter and serve.

SAVE EFFORT

Use a few pinches of dried sage if you don't have any fresh.

Serves 4

Warm Salmon and Potato Salad

Hands-on time: 15 minutes
Cooking time: about 50 minutes

750g (1lb 11oz) new potatoes, quartered

1 red onion, cut into wedges

1 tbsp olive oil

200g (7oz) cherry tomatoes

4 × 150g (5oz) salmon fillets

1 bag of watercress

salt and freshly ground black pepper

fresh basil leaves to garnish (optional)

For the dressing

juice of 1 lemon

1 tbsp wholegrain mustard

1 tbsp runny honey

50ml (2fl oz) olive oil

1 Preheat the oven to 220°C (200°C fan oven) mark 7. Put the potatoes and onion wedges into a medium roasting tin, add the oil and stir to coat. Spread the vegetables out and roast for 35 minutes or until just tender.

2 Take the tin out of the oven, stir in the cherry tomatoes and lay the salmon fillets on top of the vegetables. Season well and put back into the oven for 12 minutes more or until the fish is opaque and cooked through.

3 Meanwhile, in a small bowl, whisk together the lemon juice, mustard, honey, oil, a splash of water and plenty of seasoning until combined.

4 Empty the watercress on to a large platter or divide among four plates. Carefully slide the cooked vegetables and salmon on top. Pour the dressing over and garnish with basil, if you like.

Serves 4

Cherry Tomato and Goat's Cheese Tart

Hands-on time: 10 minutes
Cooking time: about 25 minutes

320g sheet ready-rolled puff pastry

125g (4oz) soft goat's cheese

1 tsp caster sugar

300g (11oz) cherry tomatoes, halved

1 tbsp balsamic vinegar

1 tbsp extra virgin olive oil

salt and freshly ground black pepper

a small handful of fresh basil leaves, torn, to garnish

green salad to serve

1 Preheat the oven to 220°C (200°C fan oven) mark 7. Line a baking tray with greaseproof paper.

2 Unroll the pastry sheet on to the prepared baking tray. Crumble or spread the cheese over the pastry, leaving a 1cm (½in) border around the edge. Sprinkle half the sugar over the cheese, then arrange the tomatoes on top, cut side up. Season well, then sprinkle the remaining sugar over.

3 Cook the tart for 25 minutes or until the pastry is golden and risen. Take out of the oven and drizzle with the vinegar and oil, then garnish with torn basil leaves. Serve warm or at room temperature with a green salad.

Stuffed Chicken Thighs

Hands-on time: 20 minutes
Cooking time: about 30 minutes

100g (3½oz) fresh white breadcrumbs

40g (1½oz) Parmesan, grated

2 medium eggs, lightly beaten

3 tbsp freshly chopped basil

finely grated zest of 1 lemon

8 boneless, skinless chicken thighs

8 streaky bacon rashers

salt and freshly ground black pepper

seasonal vegetables to serve

SAVE EFFORT

Use 1 tbsp dried basil if you don't have any fresh.

1 Preheat the oven to 220°C (200°C fan oven) mark 7. Put the breadcrumbs, cheese, eggs, basil, lemon zest and plenty of seasoning into a medium bowl and stir to combine.

2 Open out the chicken thighs on a board, smooth side down. Spoon half of the mixture down the centre of each, then fold the meat over the filling. Wrap a rasher of bacon around each fillet to help secure the filling in place.

3 Transfer the wrapped thighs, seam side down, to a non-stick baking tray and cook for 25–30 minutes until golden and cooked through. Serve with seasonal vegetables.

Serves 4

Lamb, Lentil and Chilli Soup

Hands-on time: 15 minutes
Cooking time: about 1 hour 40 minutes

1 tbsp vegetable oil

350g (12oz) lamb neck fillet, cut into
  small cubes

1 onion, finely chopped

2 medium carrots, finely chopped

1 celery stick, finely chopped

1 tsp ground cumin

1 tsp ground coriander

300g (11oz) yellow split peas

1.3 litres (2¼ pints) vegetable stock

1 bay leaf

salt and freshly ground black pepper

To serve

2 tbsp natural yogurt

1 red chilli, seeded and sliced into rings
  (see Safety Tip, page 34)

a small handful of fresh parsley or
  coriander leaves, chopped

crusty bread to serve

1 Heat the oil in a large pan over a medium heat and fry the lamb until nicely browned (do this in batches if necessary to stop the meat sweating). Lift the lamb out of the pan and put to one side, leaving as much oil in the pan as possible.

2 Add the chopped vegetables to the pan and cook for 5 minutes or until softened. Stir in the spices and fry for 2 minutes more. Put the lamb back into the pan with the split peas, stock and bay leaf. Bring to the boil, then reduce the heat, cover and simmer for about 1 hour 20 minutes, stirring/mashing it occasionally, until the lamb is tender and the mixture has cooked down to a fairly smooth soup.

3 Check the seasoning, adjust the consistency if you like with more stock or water and ladle into warmed bowls. Garnish with a swirl of yogurt, some fresh chilli and chopped herbs and serve with crusty bread.

Serves 4

Week 1 Shopping List

Chilled & Frozen

- ❑ 8 boneless, skinless chicken thighs
- ❑ 350g (12oz) lamb neck fillet
- ❑ 8 streaky bacon rashers
- ❑ 4 × 150g (5oz) salmon fillets
- ❑ 125g (4oz) soft goat's cheese
- ❑ 40g (1½oz) Parmesan
- ❑ 25g (1oz) butter
- ❑ Small pot natural yogurt
- ❑ 320g sheet ready-rolled puff pastry

Fruit, Vegetables & Herbs

- ❑ 2 onions
- ❑ 1 red onion
- ❑ 1 garlic bulb
- ❑ 1 red chilli
- ❑ 750g (1lb 11oz) new potatoes
- ❑ 500g (1lb 2oz) cherry tomatoes
- ❑ 2 medium carrots
- ❑ 500g (1lb 2oz) butternut squash
- ❑ 1 celery stick
- ❑ 2 lemons
- ❑ Pack of fresh sage
- ❑ Large pack of fresh basil
- ❑ Pack of fresh parsley or coriander
- ❑ 85g bag watercress
- ❑ Green salad, to serve
- ❑ Seasonal vegetables, to serve

Storecupboard
(Here's a checklist in case you need
to re-stock)

- [ ] Vegetable oil
- [ ] Olive oil
- [ ] Extra virgin olive oil
- [ ] Vegetable stock
- [ ] Balsamic vinegar
- [ ] Wholegrain mustard
- [ ] 40g (1½oz) blanched hazelnuts
- [ ] 300g (11oz) yellow split peas
- [ ] Runny honey
- [ ] Caster sugar
- [ ] 2 medium eggs
- [ ] Ground cumin
- [ ] Ground coriander
- [ ] 1 bay leaf
- [ ] 300g (11oz) risotto rice, such as
      Arborio or carnaroli
- [ ] Few slices white bread (for
      breadcrumbs)
- [ ] 50ml (2fl oz) white wine
- [ ] Crusty bread, to serve

Quick Creamy Gnocchi

Hands-on time: 10 minutes
Cooking time: about 15 minutes

2 tbsp olive oil

700g (1½lb) fresh gnocchi

200g (7oz) cream cheese

200g (7oz) frozen peas

finely grated zest of ½ lemon

2 tbsp freshly chopped chives

100–200ml (3½–7fl oz) milk, depending
on consistency

40g (1½oz) Cheddar, grated

40g (1½oz) fresh white breadcrumbs

salt and freshly ground black pepper

crisp green salad to serve

1 Preheat the grill to medium. Heat the oil in a large, deep frying pan over a high heat and add the gnocchi. Fry, stirring occasionally, until the gnocchi are turning golden and softening – about 10 minutes.

2 Stir in the cream cheese, peas, lemon zest, most of the chives, the milk and seasoning to taste (add more milk if you prefer a looser mixture). Heat through, then empty into a heatproof serving dish and sprinkle the cheese, breadcrumbs and remaining chives over the top.

3 Grill until golden and bubbling. Serve immediately with a crisp green salad.

Serves 4

Spicy Baked Eggs

Hands-on time: 15 minutes
Cooking time: about 35 minutes

1 tbsp oil

1 red onion, finely sliced

1 red chilli, seeded and finely chopped
(see Safety Tip, page 34)

1 garlic clove, crushed

2 × 400g cans chopped tomatoes

1 tsp caster sugar

400g can kidney beans, drained
and rinsed

a large handful of fresh coriander,
roughly chopped, plus extra
to garnish

8 medium eggs

salt and freshly ground black pepper

soured cream and crusty bread to serve

1. Preheat the oven to 200°C (180°C fan oven) mark 6. Heat the oil in a large frying pan and gently cook the onion for 10 minutes until softened. Stir in the chilli and garlic and cook for 1 minute more.

2. Add the tomatoes, sugar and kidney beans and simmer for 5 minutes. Stir the coriander through and check the seasoning.

3. Empty into a large, shallow, ovenproof serving dish. Make a small well in the mixture and crack an egg into it. Repeat with the remaining eggs, spacing them apart.

4. Cook in the oven for 15-20 minutes until the egg whites are set. Garnish with coriander and serve with soured cream and some crusty bread.

Barbecue Minute Steak Sandwiches

Hands-on time: 15 minutes
Cooking time: about 2 minutes

50g (2oz) butter, softened

1½ tbsp barbecue sauce

1 tbsp wholegrain mustard

4 slices taken from a white bloomer

1 tbsp olive oil

4 × minute/thin frying steaks

a large handful of rocket

3 tomatoes, sliced

1 Mix the butter, barbecue sauce and mustard together and put to one side. Toast the bread.

2 Meanwhile, heat the oil in a large frying pan over a high heat. When the pan is hot, add the steaks and cook for about 20 seconds on each side, depending on your preference.

3 Pile some rocket and tomato slices on to each piece of toast, then put a steak on top. Dollop on the barbecue butter and serve.

Serves 4

Chicken and Squash Gratin

Hands-on time: 15 minutes
Cooking time: about 50 minutes

1 tbsp vegetable oil

1 onion, finely sliced

1 leek, roughly sliced

450g (1lb) butternut squash, peeled and cut into 2.5cm (1in) pieces

3 boneless, skinless chicken breasts, cut into bite-size strips

50g (2oz) butter

50g (2oz) plain flour

500ml (17fl oz) milk

100g (3½oz) mascarpone cheese

2 tsp dried tarragon

100g (3½oz) ciabatta bread, torn into small pieces

salt and freshly ground black pepper

green salad to serve

1 Heat the oil in a large pan and gently cook the onion, leek and squash for 15 minutes, stirring occasionally, or until softened. Put to one side.

2 Meanwhile, put the chicken into a separate pan, cover with cold water and bring to the boil. Reduce the heat and simmer for 5 minutes. Drain and add to the vegetable pan.

3 Preheat the oven to 180°C (160°C fan oven) mark 4. Melt the butter in the empty pan, stir in the flour and cook for 1 minute. Take off the heat and gradually whisk in the milk to make a smooth sauce. Put back on to the heat and cook, stirring constantly, until thickened. Stir in the mascarpone and tarragon and check the seasoning. Stir the sauce into the veg and chicken pan.

4 Empty into a heatproof serving dish and top with the bread. Cook in the oven for about 30 minutes until the bread is golden and the filling is bubbling. Serve with a green salad.

Serves 4

Mustard Lamb Chops

Hands-on time: 10 minutes, plus marinating (optional)
Cooking time: about 15 minutes

3 tbsp redcurrant jelly

1 tbsp Dijon mustard

8 lamb loin chops, excess fat trimmed

salt and freshly ground black pepper

boiled or roasted new potatoes and a
  green salad to serve

For the sauce

3 tbsp mayonnaise

3 tbsp crème fraîche

1 tsp wholegrain mustard

1 Put the redcurrant jelly, mustard and seasoning to taste into a non-metallic bowl and stir to combine. Add the lamb chops and turn to make sure they are well coated. If you have time, marinate in the fridge for 1 hour.

2 Preheat the grill to medium. Arrange the chops on a non-stick baking tray and grill for 15 minutes, turning occasionally, or until the chops are golden and cooked to your liking (watch them carefully, as the sugar in the jelly can make them burn a little faster than usual). Carefully take the tray from under the grill and cover with foil. Leave to rest while you make the sauce.

3 Put the mayonnaise, crème fraîche and mustard into a small serving bowl and stir to combine. Serve the chops with the sauce, some boiled or roasted new potatoes and a green salad.

Serves 4

Week 2 Shopping List

Chilled & Frozen
- [ ] 4 × minute/thin frying steaks
- [ ] 3 boneless, skinless chicken breasts
- [ ] 8 lamb loin chops
- [ ] 700g (1½lb) fresh gnocchi
- [ ] 100g (3½oz) butter
- [ ] 700ml (1¼ pints) milk
- [ ] 100g (3½oz) mascarpone cheese
- [ ] 200g (7oz) cream cheese
- [ ] 40g (1½oz) Cheddar
- [ ] Small tub crème fraîche
- [ ] 200g (7oz) frozen peas
- [ ] Soured cream, to serve

Fruit, Vegetables & Herbs
- [ ] 1 onion
- [ ] 1 red onion
- [ ] 1 garlic bulb
- [ ] 3 tomatoes
- [ ] 1 leek
- [ ] 450g (1lb) butternut squash
- [ ] 1 red chilli
- [ ] Pack of fresh chives
- [ ] Pack of fresh coriander
- [ ] Small bag rocket
- [ ] 1 lemon
- [ ] Green salad, to serve
- [ ] New potatoes, to serve

Storecupboard
(Here's a checklist in case you need to re-stock)

- ❑ Vegetable oil
- ❑ Olive oil
- ❑ 2 × 400g cans chopped tomatoes
- ❑ Plain flour
- ❑ 400g can kidney beans
- ❑ Redcurrant jelly
- ❑ Barbecue sauce
- ❑ Wholegrain mustard
- ❑ Dijon mustard
- ❑ Mayonnaise
- ❑ Caster sugar
- ❑ 8 medium eggs
- ❑ Dried tarragon
- ❑ Few slices white bread (for breadcrumbs)
- ❑ White bloomer loaf
- ❑ Ciabatta bread
- ❑ Crusty bread, to serve

Ham, Leek and Mushroom Fusilli

Hands-on time: 10 minutes
Cooking time: about 15 minutes

350g (12oz) dried fusilli pasta

1 tbsp vegetable oil

1 leek, finely sliced

1 garlic clove, finely chopped

300g (11oz) button mushrooms, halved

200g (7oz) ham, chopped

300g (11oz) half-fat crème fraîche

a large handful of rocket

salt and freshly ground black pepper

1 Bring a large pan of salted water to the boil and cook the pasta according to the pack instructions.

2 Meanwhile, heat the oil in a large, deep frying pan and gently cook the leek for 5 minutes. Add the garlic and mushrooms and cook for 8 minutes more or until the vegetables are tender. Stir in the chopped ham and crème fraîche.

3 When the pasta is cooked to your liking, put one cupful of the cooking water to one side before draining. Stir the pasta into the sauce, then add enough of the reserved pasta water to make a smooth consistency. Season well, then add the rocket and fold through to combine. Serve immediately.

Cheesy Chicken Crispbakes

Hands-on time: 20 minutes
Cooking time: about 35 minutes

100g (3½oz) frozen peas

1kg (2¼lb) potatoes, such as Maris Piper

3 tbsp plain flour

1 medium egg, lightly beaten

4 spring onions, finely sliced

2 skinless cooked chicken breasts, finely chopped

100g (3½oz) Cheddar, grated

2 tbsp vegetable oil

salt and freshly ground black pepper

green salad to serve

1 Preheat the oven to 200°C (180°C fan oven) mark 6. Line a baking tray with baking parchment. Fill and boil a kettle. Put the peas into a colander in the sink, then pour the boiling water over them and put to one side.

2 Peel and coarsely grate the potatoes. Pile the grated potato on to a clean teatowel, gather up the corners and squeeze out as much moisture as you can. Empty the squeezed potato into a large bowl, then mix in the remaining ingredients and plenty of seasoning. Form the mixture into eight patties and arrange on the prepared baking tray.

3 Cook in the oven for 30–35 minutes until golden and cooked through. Serve with a green salad.

Serves 4

Spicy Pork Meatballs

Hands-on time: 15 minutes
Cooking time: about 35 minutes

For the meatballs

3 tbsp olive oil

400g (14oz) pork mince

½–1 red chilli, to taste, seeded and finely chopped (see Safety Tip, page 34)

½ tbsp wholegrain mustard

½ medium onion, finely chopped

1 medium egg

75g (3oz) fresh white breadcrumbs

salt and freshly ground black pepper

boiled rice to serve

For the sauce

1 tbsp olive oil

½ medium onion, finely chopped

½ tsp smoked or normal paprika

100ml (3½fl oz) red wine or beef stock

2 × 400g cans chopped tomatoes

fresh coriander or parsley to garnish (optional)

1 Preheat the oven to 200°C (180°C fan oven) mark 6. For the meatballs, pour the oil on to a lipped baking tray and put into the oven to heat up.

2 Put the mince, chilli, mustard, onion, egg, breadcrumbs and seasoning to taste into a large bowl. Use your hands to mix together, then roll into golfball-sized balls.

3 Carefully take the tray out of the oven, add the meatballs and carefully roll them to coat in the oil. Put the tray back into the oven and cook for 25 minutes, turning the balls occasionally, or until golden and cooked through.

4 Meanwhile, make the sauce. Heat the oil in a large pan and gently cook the onion for 10 minutes or until softened. Stir in the paprika and cook for 1 minute, then add the wine or stock and cook for 1 minute more. Stir in the tomatoes and leave to simmer for 15 minutes or until the sauce is thick and pulpy. Check the seasoning.

5 Add the meatballs to the tomato sauce and cook for a further 5 minutes. Garnish with coriander or parsley, if you like, and serve with rice

HEALTHY TIP

If you want to make these meatballs healthier, use turkey instead of pork mince.

Serves 4

Bean and Bacon Stew

Hands-on time: 15 minutes
Cooking time: about 50 minutes

1 tbsp vegetable oil

200g (7oz) smoked bacon lardons

1 onion, chopped

2 red peppers, seeded and roughly chopped

2 × 400g cans chopped tomatoes

a large pinch of dried chilli flakes

2 × 400g cans cannellini beans, drained and rinsed

a large handful of fresh coriander, chopped

salt and freshly ground black pepper

crusty bread to serve (optional)

1 Heat the oil in a large pan over a medium heat and fry the lardons for 5-6 minutes until golden. Lift out and put to one side, leaving the oil in the pan.

2 Add the onion, peppers and a splash of water to the pan and cook for 10 minutes or until softened. Stir in the cooked lardons, the tomatoes, chilli flakes and 200ml (7fl oz) water. Bring the mixture to the boil, then reduce the heat, cover and simmer for 20 minutes, stirring occasionally.

3 Uncover the pan, add the beans and cook for 10 minutes more. Stir in the coriander and check the seasoning. Serve with crusty bread, if you like.

SAVE EFFORT

Cannellini beans are economical, but this stew is also delicious with cans of mixed beans.

Serves 4

Beef Pilaf

Hands-on time: 10 minutes
Cooking time: about 40 minutes

1 tbsp vegetable oil

1 onion, finely sliced

450g (1lb) diced stewing beef

2 tbsp ground garam masala

200g (7oz) basmati rice

500ml (17fl oz) chicken stock

200g (7oz) fine green beans, trimmed

75g (3oz) dried apricots, chopped

4 tbsp mango chutney

salt and freshly ground black pepper

To garnish

25g (1oz) flaked almonds

freshly chopped parsley or coriander
   (optional)

1 Heat the oil in a large pan, then fry the onion for 8 minutes or until softened. Add the beef and fry for 10 minutes or until browned (add a splash of water if the pan looks too dry). Stir in the spice and rice and fry for 1 minute more.

2 Pour in the stock and bring to the boil, then reduce the heat right down, cover and simmer for 10 minutes.

3 Stir in the beans and apricots, then cover again and cook for 10 minutes more or until the stock is absorbed and the rice is tender. Fold in the chutney and season to taste. Garnish with flaked almonds and chopped parsley or coriander, if you like.

SAVE EFFORT

An easy way to get a brand new dish is to make this recipe with chopped lamb neck fillet.

Serves 4

Week 3 Shopping List

Chilled & Frozen

- [ ] 450g (1lb) diced stewing beef
- [ ] 2 skinless cooked chicken breasts
- [ ] 400g (14oz) pork mince
- [ ] 200g (7oz) smoked bacon lardons
- [ ] 200g (7oz) ham
- [ ] 300g (11oz) half-fat crème fraîche
- [ ] 100g (3½oz) Cheddar
- [ ] 100g (3½oz) frozen peas

Fruit, Vegetables & Herbs

- [ ] 3 onions
- [ ] 1 garlic bulb
- [ ] 2 red peppers
- [ ] 1kg (2¼lb) potatoes
  (such as Maris Piper)
- [ ] 300g (11oz) button mushrooms
- [ ] 1 leek
- [ ] 200g (7oz) fine green beans
- [ ] 1 red chilli
- [ ] 4 spring onions
- [ ] Pack of fresh coriander
- [ ] Pack of fresh parsley (optional)
- [ ] Pack of rocket
- [ ] Green salad, to serve

Storecupboard

(Here's a checklist in case you need
to re-stock)

- ☐ Vegetable oil
- ☐ Olive oil
- ☐ Chicken stock
- ☐ 100ml (3½fl oz) red wine or
  beef stock
- ☐ Plain flour
- ☐ 4 × 400g cans chopped tomatoes
- ☐ 2 × 400g cans cannellini beans
- ☐ Mango chutney
- ☐ Wholegrain mustard
- ☐ 2 medium eggs
- ☐ 350g (12oz) dried fusilli pasta
- ☐ Smoked or normal paprika
- ☐ Pinch of dried chilli flakes
- ☐ Ground garam masala
- ☐ Flaked almonds
- ☐ 75g (3oz) dried apricots
- ☐ 200g (7oz) basmati rice
- ☐ boiled rice, to serve
- ☐ Few slices white bread
  (for breadcrumbs)
- ☐ Crusty bread, to serve (optional)

Orange and Ginger Beef Stir-fry

Hands-on time: 15 minutes
Cooking time: about 8 minutes

1 tbsp cornflour

75ml (3fl oz) smooth orange juice

2 tbsp soy sauce

1 tbsp vegetable oil

400g (14oz) beef stir-fry strips

5cm (2in) piece fresh root ginger, peeled
and cut into matchsticks

300g pack mixed stir-fry vegetables of
your choice, chopped if large

1 tbsp sesame seeds

salt and freshly ground black pepper

egg noodles to serve

1 Put the cornflour into a small bowl
and gradually whisk in the orange
juice followed by the soy sauce to
make a smooth mixture. Put to
one side.

2 Heat the oil over a high heat in a large
frying pan or wok. Add the beef strips
and stir-fry for 1–2 minutes. Stir in the
ginger, vegetables and a splash of
water and stir-fry until the vegetables
are just tender and the beef is cooked
to your liking.

3 Add the orange juice mixture to the
pan and cook, stirring occasionally,
until thick and syrupy – about 30
seconds. Check the seasoning and
sprinkle the sesame seeds over. Serve
immediately with egg noodles.

SAVE TIME

As with all stir-fries, have your
ingredients prepared and ready to
go before you start cooking.

Serves 4

Creamy Cider Chicken

Hands-on time: 10 minutes
Cooking time: about 30 minutes

1 tbsp vegetable oil

4 boneless, skinless chicken breasts

1 medium onion, finely sliced

½ tbsp plain flour

150ml (¼ pint) cider

150ml (¼ pint) double cream

2 tbsp wholegrain mustard

a small handful of fresh parsley,
    chopped

salt and freshly ground black pepper

boiled rice or crusty bread to serve

1 Heat the oil in a large pan over a high heat and fry the chicken breasts for 5 minutes on each side or until golden. Lift the chicken out of the pan and put to one side. Add the onion to the pan and fry for 8 minutes or until softened.

2 Stir in the flour until the onions are coated, then add the cider, cream and 200ml (7fl oz) water. Put the chicken back into the pan and simmer for 12–15 minutes until cooked through (cut into one piece to make sure the meat is completely opaque).

3 Stir in the mustard and parsley and season well. Serve with boiled rice or crusty bread.

SAVE TIME

To speed up cooking time, slice the whole breasts of chicken into finger-size strips.

Crispy-crumbed Cabbage Linguine

Hands-on time: 15 minutes
Cooking time: about 15 minutes

400g (14oz) dried linguine or spaghetti

2 tbsp extra virgin olive oil

50g (2oz) fresh white breadcrumbs

300g (11oz) Savoy cabbage, shredded

2 garlic cloves, crushed

50g can anchovies in olive oil

finely grated zest of 1 lemon

a small handful of fresh parsley,
  roughly chopped

salt and freshly ground black pepper

1 Bring a large pan of salted water to the boil and cook the pasta according to the pack instructions.

2 Meanwhile, heat 1 tbsp of the oil in a large, deep frying pan. Cook the breadcrumbs, stirring frequently, until golden and crisp – about 5 minutes. Tip on to a plate and put to one side.

3 Put the frying pan back on to the heat and add the remaining oil. Stir in the cabbage and garlic and fry for 1 minute, then add two ladlefuls of pasta cooking water and cook until the cabbage is just tender. Add the anchovies with their oil and some ground black pepper, stirring to break up the fish. Put to one side.

4 Drain the pasta well and put back into the empty pan. Add the lemon zest and the cabbage mixture and toss through, then check the seasoning. Divide the linguine among four bowls and sprinkle the fried crumbs and the parsley over. Serve immediately.

Serves 4

Jarlsberg and Sweet Onion Tart

Hands-on time: 20 minutes
Cooking time: about 1 hour

plain flour to dust

375g (13oz) shortcrust pastry

1 tbsp olive oil

2 large onions, finely sliced

1 tsp caster sugar

150g (5oz) Jarlsberg cheese, finely cubed

3 medium eggs

200ml (7fl oz) double cream

2 tbsp freshly chopped chives or parsley

salt and freshly ground black pepper

green salad to serve

1 Preheat the oven to 200°C (180°C fan oven) mark 6. Lightly dust a surface with flour and roll out the pastry large enough to line a 20.5cm (8in) round, 4cm (1½in) deep, fluted tart tin. Prick the base all over with a fork.

2 Line the pastry with a sheet of baking parchment or greaseproof paper and fill with baking beans. Put the tin on a baking tray and bake blind for 15–20 minutes until the pastry sides are set.

3 While the pastry is cooking, heat the oil in a large pan and gently cook the onions for 15–20 minutes, covered, until very soft. Stir in the sugar, turn up the heat and cook, stirring frequently, until the onions are lightly caramelised. Put to one side.

4 Carefully remove the parchment and baking beans from the tin and put the pastry back into the oven. Cook for a further 10 minutes or until the base is cooked through and feels sandy to the touch. Take the tin out of the oven and reduce the oven temperature to 170°C (150°C fan oven) mark 3.

5 Spoon the onions on to the pastry base and dot the cheese over. Put the eggs into a large jug and beat lightly, then mix in the cream, herbs and plenty of seasoning. Pour over the onions and cook for 25–30 minutes until set and lightly golden. Serve warm or at room temperature with a green salad.

Smoked Haddock and Spinach Frittata

Hands-on time: 15 minutes
Cooking time: about 15 minutes

1 tbsp vegetable oil

350g (12oz) skinless smoked haddock, cut into chunks

100g bag baby spinach

8 large eggs

50ml (2fl oz) double cream

¼ tsp freshly grated nutmeg

fresh chives or parsley (optional)

50g (2oz) Cheddar, grated

freshly ground black pepper

green salad to serve

1 Heat the oil in a 23cm (9in) frying pan (suitable for use under the grill) and fry the fish, stirring occasionally, for 2 minutes. Add the spinach and cook for 3 minutes more or until wilted, trying not to break up the fish too much.

2 Preheat the grill to medium. Put the eggs, cream, nutmeg and plenty of ground black pepper into a large bowl and beat together. Add most of the chives or parsley, if you like. Pour the egg mixture into the pan and use a wooden spoon to spread it evenly between the fish. Cook over a low heat for 3–5 minutes until the egg is set around the edges.

3 Sprinkle the grated cheese over and grill for 3–5 minutes more until the egg is cooked through and the cheese is golden and bubbling. Sprinkle with the remaining herbs, if you like. Cut the frittata into wedges and serve hot or at room temperature, with a green salad.

Serves 4

Week 4 Shopping List

Chilled & Frozen

- [ ] 400g (14oz) beef stir-fry strips
- [ ] 4 boneless, skinless chicken breasts
- [ ] 350g (12oz) skinless smoked haddock
- [ ] 50g (2oz) Cheddar
- [ ] 150g (5oz) Jarlsberg cheese
- [ ] 375g (13oz) shortcrust pastry
- [ ] 400ml (14fl oz) double cream
- [ ] 75ml (3fl oz) smooth orange juice

Fruit, Vegetables & Herbs

- [ ] 1 medium onion
- [ ] 2 large onions
- [ ] 1 garlic bulb
- [ ] 5cm (2in) piece fresh root ginger
- [ ] 100g bag baby spinach
- [ ] 300g (11oz) Savoy cabbage
- [ ] 300g pack mixed stir-fry vegetables
- [ ] 1 lemon
- [ ] Pack of fresh chives (optional)
- [ ] Pack of fresh parsley
- [ ] Green salad, to serve

Storecupboard
(Here's a checklist in case you need to re-stock)

- ❑ Vegetable oil
- ❑ Olive oil
- ❑ Extra virgin olive oil
- ❑ Plain flour
- ❑ 50g can anchovies in olive oil
- ❑ Soy sauce
- ❑ Wholegrain mustard
- ❑ 3 medium eggs
- ❑ 8 large eggs
- ❑ 400g (14oz) dried linguine or spaghetti
- ❑ Caster sugar
- ❑ Cornflour
- ❑ Nutmeg
- ❑ Sesame seeds
- ❑ A few slices white bread (for breadcrumbs)
- ❑ 150ml (¼ pint) cider
- ❑ Crusty bread, to serve
- ❑ Egg noodles, to serve
- ❑ Rice, to serve (optional)

Impress your Guests for a Fiver

Planning Ahead

Planning will make your life easier when you're shopping on a budget. Unlike our grandmothers, who shopped daily and often only had a pantry for storage, we have the fridge and freezer alongside our storecupboard.

Savvy shopping

Clever use of the fridge, freezer and storecupboard makes life easier and shopping trips fewer. Nowadays, Sunday's roast doesn't have to be Monday's cottage pie if it's prepared and put in the freezer for another day.

Change your shopping habits

❑ Do a big supermarket shop once a month for non-perishables – even better, order your shopping on-line to avoid impulse buys and keep an eye on the running total before you place the order. Some delivery companies offer free delivery at less popular times

❑ Top up with daily or weekly shops at supermarkets, independent shops or street markets for fresh ingredients

❑ Only buy special offers or BOGOFs (buy one, get one free) if you have time to batch cook or space to freeze the extra

❑ Avoid ready-meals and ready-prepared ingredients, such as chopped onions – you are paying more for convenience

Before you go shopping

❑ Can you delay your food shop for another day? Check the storecupboard, fridge or freezer for ingredients that can make another meal

❑ Check the diary and plan the week's menu according to family activities

❑ Do a quick weekly stock-take of the storecupboard, fridge and freezer. Can ingredients near their use-by or best-before date be incorporated into the week's menu?

❑ Don't forget nature's free storecupboard – blackberries in hedgerows, sweet chestnuts and sloes, for example

The weekly menu

This needn't be a hefty document, simply jot down:

- ❏ An idea for every day of the week, including some dishes that you've already made and stored in the fridge or freezer
- ❏ Some recipes that make creative use of leftovers
- ❏ Some recipes that stretch – bolognese tonight, chilli tomorrow
- ❏ Some quick meals that need a trip to the shops for one or two fresh ingredients
- ❏ Include vegetables or other accompaniments in your plan, but remember that you can always change your mind if you find a bargain in the supermarket
- ❏ Rethink your approach to cooking – meat and fish are expensive, so you could make one or two nights a week vegetarian, if you like

When you're shopping

- ❏ Tuck a notebook in your bag listing ingredients for family favourites and you'll be ready to take advantage of special offers on expensive ingredients such as meat and poultry
- ❏ Make a shopping list and stick to it
- ❏ Keep it seasonal (see pages 8–11)
- ❏ Does the product cost less whole or in portions – for example, it's cheaper to:
  - buy a whole chicken and joint it into pieces yourself (or ask your butcher to do it). Use the carcass for stock
  - cut a whole salmon into fillets or steaks, then freeze in portions
- ❏ Compare the price per kilo. Loose fruit and vegetables can cost considerably less than pre-packed versions, for example

Macaroni Cheese

Hands-on time: 15 minutes
Cooking time: about 20 minutes

450g (1lb) macaroni pasta
40g (1½oz) butter
40g (1½oz) plain flour
500ml (17fl oz) semi-skimmed milk
125g (4oz) mature Cheddar, grated
25g (1oz) fresh white breadcrumbs
salt and freshly ground black pepper
green salad to serve

1 Bring a large pan of salted water to the boil and cook the macaroni pasta for 5–8 minutes until just tender. Drain.

2 Meanwhile, melt the butter in a large pan. Stir in the flour and cook for 1 minute. Take off the heat and gradually beat in the milk using a wooden spoon. Heat gently, stirring constantly, until the mixture thickens – 3–5 minutes. Take off the heat, stir in 75g (3oz) of the cheese and the drained macaroni. Check the seasoning.

3 Preheat the grill to medium. Empty the macaroni mixture into a 2 litre (3½ pint) ovenproof serving dish and top with the remaining cheese and the breadcrumbs. Grill for about 5 minutes until piping hot and golden. Serve immediately with a green salad.

Mushroom Linguine

Hands-on time: 10 minutes
Cooking time: about 10 minutes

400g (14oz) linguine

15g (½oz) butter

350g (12oz) chestnut mushrooms, sliced

25g (1oz) pinenuts

1 tbsp brandy (optional)

100g (3½oz) mascarpone cheese

40g (1½oz) Parmesan, grated, plus extra
    to garnish

finely grated zest of 1 lemon

a large handful of baby spinach

salt and freshly ground black pepper

1 Cook the linguine according to the
   pack instructions. Drain, keeping
   150ml (¼ pint) of the cooking water to
   one side.

2 Meanwhile, heat the butter in a large
   frying pan over a high heat. Add the
   mushrooms and cook for 3–5 minutes.
   Add the pinenuts and cook for 1
   minute. Stir in the brandy, if you like,
   and bubble for 1 minute.

3 Add the mascarpone, Parmesan,
   reserved cooking water and lemon
   zest to the pan, then stir in the spinach
   and linguine and heat through. Check
   the seasoning, garnish with extra
   Parmesan and serve.

Serves 4

Fish, Chips and Mashed Minted Peas

Hands-on time: 15 minutes
Cooking time: about 40 minutes

4 large baking potatoes, about
   900g (2lb)

3 tbsp vegetable oil

25g (1oz) plain flour

1 large egg, beaten

100g (3½oz) fresh white breadcrumbs

4 × 125g (4oz) cod fillets, skinned

450g (1lb) fresh or frozen peas

1½ tbsp finely sliced fresh mint

salt and freshly ground black pepper

tartare sauce, lemon wedges and malt
   vinegar to serve

1 Preheat the oven to 200°C (180°C fan oven) mark 6. Cut the potatoes into wedges and put on a large baking tray. Drizzle with 1½ tbsp of the oil, season well and toss to coat the wedges. Cook in the oven for 30–40 minutes until tender and golden brown.

2 Put the flour, egg and breadcrumbs on to three separate lipped plates.

3 When the wedges are 10 minutes away from being finished, bring a medium pan of water to the boil. Meanwhile, coat each fish fillet in flour, tapping off the excess, then dip into the egg and then into the breadcrumbs.

4 Heat the remaining 1½ tbsp oil in a large, non-stick frying pan and cook the fish for 5 minutes, turning once, or until golden brown and cooked through.

5 Add the peas to the boiling water and cook for 2–3 minutes until tender. Drain. Using a potato masher, roughly crush the peas, then stir in the mint and seasoning to taste. Serve the fish immediately with a dollop of tartare sauce and a lemon wedge, plus the potato wedges and peas, and malt vinegar to sprinkle over.

Frozen fish fillets keep costs down.
It's best to thaw them fully before
using – in the fridge on a baking
tray lined with lots of kitchen paper
is ideal.

Serves 4

Keep It Low Cost

It can be hard making sure that every member of the family eats healthy and balanced meals, especially if they come home at different times after various activities. Planning each week's menu in advance not only takes the stress out of deciding what to cook each day, but can save you money long term.

Avoiding waste

By checking storecupboards, planning your weekly menu and always shopping with a list, you are well on your way to avoiding waste in the kitchen, as well as saving money. But it's inevitable that there will be some leftovers from time to time; for example, if last-minute plans prevent you eating a supper that has already been planned for the week. A regular check of use-by dates of ingredients in the fridge should prevent this and planning ahead will help you to use them up in quick suppers or dishes to freeze for another day.

Expiry dates

These are a major area of debate. Supermarkets are extremely strict on expiry dates and will throw out any food the moment it is 'out of date'. Once you have purchased a product, you are asked to use it within the 'use by' date. After this, you are encouraged to throw it out and start again. However, with the odd exception – and using your judgement on certain danger foods like fish and chicken – you can simply check if it's okay to use by smell, look and feel. Follow your instincts: if it smells bad, bin it.

Portion sizes (per person)

As a rough guide, vegetables should half-fill the plate, while meat, fish or poultry should take up one quarter, with the remainder filled with carbohydrates, such as rice, pasta or potatoes.

Soup	300ml (½ pint)

Fish, poultry and meat

off the bone	175g (6oz)

Whole chicken,	1.4kg (3lb)
leg of lamb or pork	

should serve four with leftovers

Casseroles, stews

trimmed meat	225g (8oz)

Shellfish

as main course	125g (4oz)

Vegetables

· assuming you are serving three vegetables	50g (2oz)
· assuming you are serving two vegetables	75g (3oz)

Potatoes

small roast	3
mashed	175g (6oz)
new	125g (4oz)

Rice (as an accompaniment)

pre-cooked weight	50g (2oz)

Couscous and bulgur wheat (as an accompaniment)

pre-cooked weight	50g (2oz)

Dried pasta	75–100g (3–3½oz)

Salads	1 dessert bowl

Quick Carbonara

Hands-on time: 10 minutes
Cooking time: about 15 minutes

350g (12oz) dried linguine

½ tbsp olive oil

200g (7oz) unsmoked bacon lardons

4 large eggs

75g (3oz) freshly grated Parmesan, plus extra to serve

freshly ground black pepper

chopped fresh parsley to garnish

SAVE MONEY

This timeless recipe is usually made with cream, but this authentic version uses pasta cooking water for a meal that's lighter on your purse.

1 Bring a large pan of water to the boil and cook the linguine according to the pack instructions.

2 Meanwhile, heat the oil in a large frying pan and fry the lardons for 5 minutes or until golden. Take the pan off the heat.

3 Beat the eggs in a medium bowl with the Parmesan and plenty of ground black pepper. Drain the pasta, keeping 100ml (3½fl oz) of the cooking water to one side. Put the bacon pan back on to a low heat and stir in the pasta water, pasta and egg mixture. Stir for 1 minute or until thickened. Check the seasoning, garnish with a small handful of parsley and extra Parmesan and serve.

Serves 4

Beef Quesadillas

Hands-on time: 15 minutes
Cooking time: about 45 minutes

½ tbsp vegetable oil

5 spring onions, finely sliced

400g (14oz) lean beef mince

a few dashes of Tabasco

¼ tsp paprika

1 garlic clove, finely sliced

2 × 400g cans chopped tomatoes

8 flour tortillas

125g (4oz) mature Cheddar, grated

a large handful of fresh coriander,
   roughly chopped

salt and freshly ground black pepper

lime wedges and soured cream to serve

1 Heat the oil in a large frying pan. Fry the spring onions for 3–5 minutes until just softened. Empty into a large bowl. Brown the beef in the same pan over a high heat for 5 minutes or until cooked through. Stir in the Tabasco, paprika and garlic and cook for 1 minute. Add the tomatoes and seasoning to taste and simmer for 10 minutes. Tip the beef mixture into the bowl with the spring onions.

2 Wipe the pan clean, then put back on to a medium heat. Put a tortilla in the pan, then spoon on a quarter each of the beef mixture, cheese and coriander. Top with another tortilla and heat through for 3 minutes.

3 Using a spatula, flip the quesadilla and cook on the other side for 3 minutes. Slide on to a board, then cover with foil. Repeat with the remaining tortillas. Serve quartered, with lime wedges and soured cream.

Serves 4

Swedish Meatballs

Hands-on time: 15 minutes
Cooking time: about 15 minutes

500g (1lb 2oz) pork mince
1 tbsp wholegrain mustard
1 large egg
75g (3oz) fresh white breadcrumbs
3 tbsp finely chopped fresh dill
1 tbsp vegetable oil
300ml (½ pint) chicken stock
150ml (¼ pint) double cream
salt and freshly ground black pepper
cranberry sauce and boiled basmati rice
  to serve

1 Put the pork, mustard, egg,
  breadcrumbs, 2 tbsp of the dill and
  seasoning to taste into a large bowl
  and mix well. Form into 20 golfball-
  size balls.

2 Heat the oil in a large frying pan over
  a medium heat. Fry the meatballs for
  8–10 minutes until cooked through
  and golden.

3 Pour in the stock and cream, bring
  to the boil and bubble for 3 minutes.
  Sprinkle in the remaining dill and
  check the seasoning. Serve with
  cranberry sauce and rice.

Serves 4

Pork Schnitzel

Hands-on time: 15 minutes
Cooking time: about 5 minutes

4 pork loin steaks, thin-cut

25g (1oz) plain flour

2 medium eggs, beaten

150g (5oz) fresh white breadcrumbs

2 tbsp sunflower oil

1 lemon, cut into wedges

green salad to serve

SAVE EFFORT

For an easy variation on this
Austrian favourite, just substitute
chicken or turkey breasts, flattened.

1. Put one steak on to a board and cover with clingfilm. Using a rolling pin, gently hit the pork and flatten to an even thickness of 0.5cm (¼in). Peel off the clingfilm and leave the pork to dry on some kitchen paper. Repeat with the remaining steaks.

2. Put the flour, eggs and breadcrumbs on to three separate lipped plates. Coat each steak in flour, tapping off the excess, then dip into the beaten eggs followed by the breadcrumbs.

3. Heat the oil in a large non-stick frying pan and fry the breaded steaks for 5 minutes, turning once, until golden and cooked through. Serve with lemon wedges and a green salad.

Serves 4

Sweet and Sour Pork Stir-fry

Hands-on time: 15 minutes
Cooking time: about 10 minutes

2 tbsp vegetable oil

350g (12oz) pork fillet, cut into
finger-size pieces

1 red onion, finely sliced

1 red pepper, seeded and finely sliced

2 carrots, cut into thin strips

3 tbsp sweet chilli sauce

1 tbsp white wine vinegar

220g can pineapple slices, chopped, with
2 tbsp juice put to one side

a large handful of bean sprouts

½ tbsp sesame seeds

a large handful of fresh coriander,
roughly chopped

salt and freshly ground black pepper

boiled long-grain rice to serve

1 Heat the oil over a high heat in a
large frying pan or wok. Add the
pork, onion, red pepper and carrots
and cook for 3–5 minutes, stirring
frequently, until the meat is cooked
through and the vegetables are
softening.

2 Stir in the chilli sauce, vinegar
and reserved pineapple juice and
bring to the boil, then stir in the
pineapple chunks and bean sprouts
and heat through.

3 Check the seasoning. Scatter the
sesame seeds and coriander over
and serve immediately with rice.

SAVE TIME

As with all stir-fries, have
everything sliced and ready
before you start cooking.

Serves 4

Quick Curry

Hands-on time: 10 minutes
Cooking time: about 10 minutes

1 tbsp sunflower oil

1 medium onion, finely sliced

100g (3½oz) chorizo, skinned and finely cubed or sliced

1 garlic clove, crushed

1 red chilli, seeded and finely sliced (see Safety Tip, page 34)

1 tsp ground garam masala

160ml can coconut cream

2 × 400g can chickpeas, drained and rinsed

a large handful of spinach

salt and freshly ground black pepper

boiled basmati rice to serve

1 Heat the oil in a large pan and gently fry the onion for 5 minutes or until softened. Add the chorizo, garlic and chilli and cook for 2 minutes or until the chorizo is golden. Stir in the garam masala and cook for 1 minute.

2 Add the coconut cream, chickpeas and 200ml (7fl oz) water and heat through. Stir in the spinach and check the seasoning. Serve immediately with rice.

Serves 4

Chicken Kiev

Hands-on time: 15 minutes
Cooking time: about 25 minutes

50g (2oz) butter, softened

½ garlic clove, crushed

2 tbsp finely chopped fresh parsley

4 chicken breasts

40g (1½oz) plain flour

3 medium eggs, beaten

200g (7oz) fine fresh white breadcrumbs

salt and freshly ground black pepper

cocktail sticks

green salad to serve

1 Preheat the oven to 200°C (180°C fan oven) mark 6. Mix the butter with the garlic, parsley and seasoning to taste. Cut a slit 4cm (1½in) long and 1cm (½in) deep in the top of each chicken breast. Press one-quarter of the butter mixture into each slit and secure with a cocktail stick.

2 Put the flour, eggs and breadcrumbs on to three separate lipped plates. Coat each chicken breast in flour, tapping off the excess, then dip into the eggs and then into the breadcrumbs. Finish by dipping each breast into the egg again before coating with a final layer of breadcrumbs.

3 Put the breaded chicken breasts on a baking tray and cook for 20–25 minutes until cooked through. Remove the cocktail sticks and serve immediately with green salad.

Serves 4

Chicken Tagine

Hands-on time: 15 minutes
Cooking time: about 25 minutes

1 tbsp vegetable oil

8 chicken drumsticks

½ tsp each ground cumin, coriander,
   cinnamon and paprika

75g (3oz) ready-to-eat dried apricots,
   finely chopped

40g (1½oz) raisins

400g can chopped tomatoes

75g (3oz) couscous

salt and freshly ground black pepper

a large handful of fresh coriander,
   chopped, to garnish

1 Heat the oil in a large flameproof
   casserole and brown the drumsticks
   well all over. Stir in the spices and
   cook for 1 minute. Add the apricots,
   raisins, tomatoes, 400ml (14fl oz)
   water and seasoning to taste, bring to
   the boil, and simmer for 10 minutes.

2 Stir in the couscous and simmer for
   5 minutes more or until the couscous
   is tender and the chicken is cooked
   through. Check the seasoning.
   Sprinkle with chopped coriander and
   serve immediately.

Serves 4

Jerk Chicken

Hands-on time: 10 minutes
Cooking time: about 15 minutes

1 tbsp fresh thyme leaves

2.5cm (1in) piece fresh root ginger, peeled and grated

1 tsp ground allspice

1 tbsp white wine vinegar

1 tsp soy sauce

1 garlic clove, crushed

2 green chillies, seeded and finely chopped (see Safety Tip, page 34)

3 tbsp vegetable oil

8 chicken pieces, such as thighs and drumsticks

boiled basmati rice and a green salad or seasonal vegetables to serve

1 Preheat the grill to medium and set the grill rack about 15cm (6in) from the heat. Use a blender or a pestle and mortar to combine the thyme, ginger, allspice, vinegar, soy sauce, garlic, chillies and oil until smooth.

2 Put the chicken pieces on to a foil-lined baking sheet, then pour the jerk marinade over them and rub into the chicken. Grill for 12–15 minutes until golden and cooked through. Serve with rice and a green salad or seasonal vegetables.

Serves 4

Paella

1 tbsp vegetable oil

1 large onion, thinly sliced

4 boneless, skinless chicken thighs, roughly chopped

2 garlic cloves, finely chopped

a pinch of saffron

¼ tsp smoked paprika

1 red pepper, seeded and finely diced

300g (11oz) paella rice

1.1 litres (2 pints) hot chicken stock

180g tub mussel meat, drained if in brine

a large handful of fresh curly parsley, roughly chopped

salt and freshly ground black pepper

1 Gently heat the oil in a large paella pan or frying pan and cook the onion for 5 minutes. Add the chicken and cook for 3 minutes. Stir in the garlic, saffron and paprika and cook for 1 minute to release the flavours.

2 Stir in the red pepper and rice. Pour in the hot stock and leave to simmer gently for 20 minutes, stirring occasionally, or until the rice is cooked through.

3 Stir in the mussels and parsley and check the seasoning. Serve immediately.

Serves 4

From the
Storecupboard

A Well-stocked Storecupboard

A well-stocked storecupboard can help you rustle up a quick meal at short notice. However, resist the urge to fill the cupboard with interesting bottles that you 'might use one day'.

Stocking your storecupboard

Dried

- ❑ Pasta and noodles
- ❑ Rice (long-grain, Arborio and other risotto rice, pudding rice)
- ❑ Pulses
- ❑ Pizza bases
- ❑ Nuts (pinenuts, walnuts, almonds)
- ❑ Dried fruits
- ❑ Stock cubes
- ❑ Spices and herbs
- ❑ Salt and ground black pepper
- ❑ Flour (plain, self-raising, wholemeal and cornflour)
- ❑ Dried yeast
- ❑ Gelatine
- ❑ Baking powder, cream of tartar, bicarbonate of soda
- ❑ Sugar
- ❑ Tea
- ❑ Coffee
- ❑ Cocoa powder

Bottles and jars

- ❑ Mayonnaise
- ❑ Tomato ketchup and purée
- ❑ Tabasco sauce
- ❑ Worcestershire sauce
- ❑ Sweet chilli sauce
- ❑ Pasta sauces
- ❑ Thai fish sauce
- ❑ Curry paste
- ❑ Chutneys
- ❑ Pickles
- ❑ Olives
- ❑ Capers
- ❑ Mustards
- ❑ Oils
- ❑ Vinegar
- ❑ Jam
- ❑ Marmalade
- ❑ Honey

Cans

- ☐ Chopped and whole tomatoes
- ☐ Fish (salmon, tuna, anchovies)
- ☐ Beans, chickpeas and lentils
- ☐ Coconut milk/cream
- ☐ Fruits

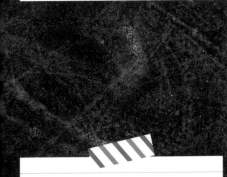

Variations

- Use 100g (3½oz) sun-dried tomatoes instead of the new potatoes.
- Throw in a handful of halved pitted black olives as you pour the egg into the pan.

Storecupboard Recipes

Storecupboard Omelette

A drizzle of olive oil or knob of butter, 1 large onion, finely chopped, 225g (8oz) cooked new potatoes, sliced, 125g (4oz) frozen petit pois, thawed, 6 medium eggs, beaten, 150g pack soft goat's cheese, sliced, salt and freshly ground black pepper.

1   Heat the oil or butter in a 25.5cm (10in) non-stick, ovenproof frying pan. Add the onion and fry for 6–8 minutes until golden. Add the potatoes and petit pois and cook, stirring, for 2–3 minutes. Preheat the grill.

2   Spread the mixture over the base of the pan and pour in the eggs. Tilt the pan to coat the base with egg. Leave the omelette to cook undisturbed for 2–3 minutes, then top with the cheese.

3   Put the pan under the hot grill for 1–2 minutes until the egg is just set (no longer, or it will turn rubbery) and the cheese starts to turn golden. Season with salt and ground black pepper and serve.

Salmon and Pea Fishcakes

🍴 **Hands-on time:** 15 minutes
Cooking time: about 10 minutes

100g (3½oz) frozen peas

15 cream crackers, about 125g (4oz)

2 × 180g cans boneless, skinless salmon, drained

1 medium egg, separated

a few drops of Tabasco, to taste

1 tbsp freshly chopped dill

1 tbsp vegetable oil

3 tbsp mayonnaise

2 tbsp sweet chilli sauce

salt and freshly ground black pepper

green salad to serve

1 Put the peas into a bowl, cover with boiling water and leave for a few minutes. Meanwhile, put five of the cream crackers into a food processor and whiz until fine. Tip on to a shallow plate and put to one side for the coating. Next, whiz the remaining whole crackers until fine. Add the salmon, egg yolk, Tabasco, dill and plenty of seasoning to the processor and whiz again until combined.

Drain the peas and add to the salmon mixture, then pulse briefly to combine.

2 Put the egg white into a shallow bowl and whisk lightly with a fork to break it up. Shape the fish mixture into four patties. Dip each one into the egg white, then coat in the reserved cracker crumbs.

3 Heat the oil in a large frying pan and cook the fishcakes for 5 minutes on each side or until golden and piping hot.

4 Meanwhile, stir the mayonnaise and chilli sauce together in a small bowl. Serve the fishcakes with the dipping sauce and a green salad.

SAVE EFFORT

Cream crackers are an excellent substitute for breadcrumbs and help to bind these easy fishcakes.

Serves 4

Penne Puttanesca

Hands-on time: 10 minutes
Cooking time: about 25 minutes

350g (12oz) dried penne pasta

1 tbsp olive oil

1 onion, finely chopped

400g can chopped tomatoes

2 tsp dried oregano

120g can boneless, skinless sardine
 fillets, drained

50g (2oz) black olives, pitted

salt and freshly ground black pepper

a small handful of fresh curly parsley,
 chopped, to garnish

SAVE EFFORT

Sardines give this dish substance
and texture, but in their place,
and to get a different dish, try
anchovies, the classic addition,
for their salty oomph.

1 Bring a large pan of salted water to
 the boil and cook the pasta according
 to the pack instructions. Strain well,
 keeping a cupful of the cooking water
 to one side.

2 Meanwhile, heat the oil in a large pan
 and fry the onion for 10 minutes or
 until softened but not coloured. Add
 the tomatoes and oregano, then bring
 the mixture to the boil, reduce the
 heat and simmer for 15 minutes until
 thickened. Stir in the sardines and
 olives – the stirring should help break
 up the fish slightly.

3 Add the pasta to the sauce and toss
 well to combine. Add a little of the
 reserved pasta water if the mixture
 looks too dry. Check the seasoning,
 then divide among four bowls
 and garnish with parsley. Serve
 immediately.

Serves 4

Cheesy Chicken and Vegetable Cobbler

Hands-on time: 20 minutes
Cooking time: about 20 minutes

200g (7oz) cooked skinless chicken breast, cut into bite-size pieces

200g (7oz) frozen mixed vegetables

300g can cream of tomato soup

175g (6oz) self-raising flour, plus extra to dust

½ tbsp baking powder

50g (2oz) mature Cheddar, grated

75ml (3fl oz) milk, plus extra to brush

1 medium egg, lightly beaten

½ tbsp vegetable oil

salt and freshly ground black pepper

1 Preheat the oven to 200°C (180°C fan oven) mark 6. Put the cooked chicken, frozen vegetables, soup and seasoning to taste into a medium bowl and stir to combine. Pour the mixture into a (roughly) 1 litre (1¾ pint) shallow, ovenproof dish and put to one side.

2 Sift the flour, baking powder and a large pinch of salt into a large bowl. Stir in most of the cheese. Beat the milk, egg and oil together in a separate bowl.

3 Pour the milk mixture into the flour bowl and use a cutlery knife to bring it together until the dough forms clumps. Add a splash of milk if it looks too dry.

4 Tip the dough out on to a lightly floured worksurface and pat it into a (roughly) 9 × 15cm (3½ × 6in) rectangle. Cut the rectangle into eight equal squares, then arrange the scones on top of the chicken mixture. Brush each scone with a little milk, then sprinkle the remaining cheese on top.

5 Cook in the oven for 20 minutes or until the scones are risen and golden and the filling is bubbling and piping hot. Serve immediately.

132

Serves 4

Make Your Own Stock

Good stock can make the difference between a good dish and a great one. It gives depth of flavour to many dishes. There are four main types of stock: vegetable, meat, chicken and fish.

Vegetable Stock

For 1.1 litres (2 pints), you will need: 225g (8oz) each chopped onion, celery, leek and carrot, 2 bay leaves, a few fresh thyme sprigs, 1 small bunch of fresh parsley, 10 black peppercorns, ½ tsp salt.

1 Put all the ingredients into a pan and pour in 1.7 litres (3 pints) cold water.
2 Bring slowly to the boil and skim the surface. Reduce the heat, partially cover the pan and simmer gently for 30 minutes. Adjust the seasoning if necessary.
3 Strain the stock through a fine sieve into a bowl and leave to cool.

Chicken Stock

For 1.1 litres (2 pints), you will need: 1.6kg (3½lb) chicken bones or a stripped roast chicken carcass, 225g (8oz) each sliced onions and celery, 150g (5oz) chopped leeks, 1 bouquet garni (2 bay leaves, a few fresh thyme sprigs and a small bunch of fresh parsley), 1 tsp black peppercorns, ½ tsp salt.

1 Put all the ingredients into a large pan with 3 litres (5¼ pints) cold water.
2 Bring slowly to the boil and skim the surface. Reduce the heat, partially cover the pan and simmer gently for 2 hours. Adjust the seasoning if necessary.
3 Strain the stock through a muslin-lined sieve into a bowl and cool quickly. Degrease (see opposite) before using.

Fish Stock

For 900ml (1½ pints), you will need: 900g (2lb) washed fish bones and trimmings, 2 chopped carrots, 1 chopped onion and 2 sliced celery sticks, 1 bouquet garni (2 bay leaves, a few fresh thyme sprigs and a small bunch of fresh parsley), 6 white peppercorns, ½ tsp salt.

1. Put all the ingredients into a large pan with 900ml (1½ pints) cold water.
2. Bring slowly to the boil and skim the surface. Reduce the heat, partially cover the pan and simmer gently for 30 minutes. Adjust the seasoning if necessary.
3. Strain the stock through a muslin-lined sieve into a bowl and cool quickly. Fish stock tends not to have much fat in it and so does not usually need to be degreased. However, if it does seem to be fatty, you will need to remove this by degreasing it (see right).

Degreasing stock

Meat and poultry stock needs to be degreased. (Vegetable stock does not.) You can mop the fat from the surface using kitchen paper, but the following methods are easier and more effective. There are three main methods that you can use: ladling, pouring and chilling.

1. **Ladling** While the stock is warm, place a ladle on the surface. Press down to allow the fat floating on the surface to trickle over the edge until the ladle is full. Discard the fat, then repeat until all the fat has been removed.
2. **Pouring** For this you need a degreasing jug or a double-pouring gravy boat, which has the spout at the bottom of the vessel. When you fill the jug or gravy boat with a fatty liquid, the fat rises. When you pour, the stock comes out while the fat stays behind in the jug.
3. **Chilling** This technique works best with stock made from meat, whose fat solidifies when cold. Put the stock in the fridge until the fat becomes solid, then remove the pieces of fat using a slotted spoon.

Steak and Guinness Pie

Hands-on time: 20 minutes
Cooking time: about 1 hour 25 minutes

400g (14oz) braising steak, cut into 2cm (¾in) cubes

25g (1oz) plain flour, plus extra to dust

1 tbsp vegetable oil

2 medium carrots, roughly chopped

1 onion, finely sliced

250ml (9fl oz) Guinness

250ml (9fl oz) beef stock

50ml (2fl oz) double cream

1 tbsp redcurrant jelly

a small handful of fresh flat-leafed parsley, finely chopped

300g (11oz) puff pastry

salt and freshly ground black pepper

1 Put the steak into a bowl and coat with the flour. Heat the oil in a 3.4 litre (6 pint) flameproof casserole and brown the beef, in batches if necessary to stop the meat sweating. Add the carrots and onion and cook for 3 minutes. Stir in the Guinness and stock and season to taste. Bring to the boil, then reduce the heat, cover and simmer for 30–40 minutes until the beef is tender, uncovering for the last 10 minutes.

2 Preheat the oven to 220°C (200°C fan oven) mark 7. Stir the cream, redcurrant jelly and parsley into the beef mixture and check the seasoning. Put to one side.

3 Dust a worksurface with flour and roll out the pastry to the thickness of a £1 coin. Use the pastry to cover the casserole, laying it on top of the beef mixture, then make a small slit in the middle of the pastry to allow the steam to escape. Cook in the oven for 25–30 minutes until the pastry is a deep golden brown. Serve immediately.

Serves 4

Quorn Lasagne

Hands-on time: 15 minutes
Cooking time: about 1 hour

3 tbsp olive oil

1 onion, finely chopped

2 × 300g bags frozen Quorn mince

100ml (3½fl oz) red wine

2 × 400g cans chopped tomatoes

1½ tbsp mixed dried herbs

½ vegetable stock cube

4 tbsp plain flour

600ml (1 pint) milk

9 dried and ready to cook lasagne sheets

50g (2oz) mature Cheddar, grated

salt and freshly ground black pepper

green salad to serve

1 Heat 1 tbsp of the oil in a large pan and fry the onion for 10 minutes or until softened. Turn up the heat, add the Quorn and fry for 5 minutes or until golden. Add the wine and simmer for 5 minutes.

2 Stir in the tomatoes and mixed herbs, then crumble in the stock cube and seasoning to taste. Bring the mixture to the boil, then reduce the heat and simmer for 5 minutes or until thickened. Take off the heat.

3 Next, make the white sauce. Heat the remaining oil in a small pan and stir in the flour. Cook for 30 seconds, then take the pan off the heat and gradually whisk in the milk. Put the milk mixture back on to the heat and bring to the boil, then reduce the heat and simmer for 5 minutes, whisking constantly, or until thickened and glossy.

4 Preheat the oven to 200°C (180°C fan oven) mark 6. Spoon a third of the mince mixture into the bottom of a 2 litre (3½ pint) ovenproof dish. Cover with three lasagne sheets and a little white sauce. Repeat the layering process twice more, finishing with a layer of white sauce. Sprinkle the cheese over and cook in the oven for 30–35 minutes until bubbling and golden (cover with foil if browning too quickly). Serve with a green salad.

Sticky Ribs with Rice and Beans

Hands-on time: 15 minutes
Cooking time: about 55 minutes

125g (4oz) tomato ketchup

1½ tbsp soy sauce

1½ tbsp white wine vinegar

3 tbsp runny honey

1½ tsp mixed spice

½ tsp hot chilli powder

1.5kg (3lb 2oz) individual pork spare ribs

250g (9oz) basmati rice

400g can kidney beans, drained and rinsed

a large handful of fresh coriander, chopped

green salad to serve

1. Preheat the oven to 200°C (180°C fan oven) mark 6. Line a large roasting tin with a double layer of foil. Put the first six ingredients into a large bowl and stir to combine. Add the ribs to the bowl and stir to coat completely, then empty the ribs and glaze into the prepared roasting tin and spread out evenly. Cover with foil and cook for 20 minutes.

2. Uncover the tin, then turn the ribs and put back into the oven for 30–35 minutes, turning in the glaze occasionally, until they're dark and sticky (most of the liquid should have evaporated).

3. Meanwhile, cook the rice according to the pack instructions, adding the kidney beans for the final 2 minutes of cooking. Drain well and stir in the coriander. Serve the rice with the ribs and a green salad.

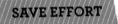

SAVE EFFORT

An easy way to get a different dish is to use this delicious glaze on grilled sausages or sizzling pork.

Serves 4

Before doing your weekly shop, have a good look at the ingredients in your fridge and vegetable rack and think of ways to use them up. You can then go out and buy the ingredients you need to make the most of the items you already have.

Clever leftovers

We all struggle with portion sizing and often have extra rice, potatoes or other ingredients left at the end of each meal. There is a difference between leftovers and waste food. Leftovers are the bits and pieces that sit in a clingfilm-covered bowl in your fridge, challenging you to use them creatively. If you ignore them for four or five days they become waste. Why not try making the most of your leftover bits and bobs?

Ways of using leftovers

There are many ways of using leftover food and slightly over-ripe fruit and vegetables that are starting to wilt. You can:

❑ Simply add the ingredients to a stir-fry, pasta bake, soup, risotto… the list is endless

❑ 'Stretch' the ingredients – sometimes the amount left over is so small it won't go very far in a family setting. Try adding to it. You can cook a little more of it (for example, rice), or try adding lentils and tomatoes to leftover mince to create a whole new take on Bolognese sauce

❑ Make the most of fruit and vegetables that are starting to wilt – use fruit in a crumble, use vegetables in soups and bakes

Alternative suggestions

You may not always feel like transforming your leftovers into meals – or there may not be enough to do so. Another option is to freeze the odd ingredient for later use.

Small amounts of herbs – freeze in ice cube trays

One or two chillies – these freeze well and are easy to chop from frozen

Double cream – lightly whip the cream and then freeze

Cheese – hard cheeses will become crumbly once thawed, but can be used for grating or in cooking

Bread – whiz in a food processor to make breadcrumbs: these freeze well in a sealed plastic bag. Use to sprinkle over bakes for a crisp topping, or to coat fish or chicken before frying, grilling or baking – or use for bread sauce to serve with game or turkey

Leftover Roast Chicken Soup

3 tbsp olive oil, 1 chopped onion, 1 chopped carrot, 2 chopped celery sticks, 2 chopped fresh thyme sprigs, 1 bay leaf, a stripped roast chicken carcass, 150-200g (5-7oz) chopped roast chicken, 200g (7oz) mashed or roast potato, 1 tbsp double cream, salt and freshly ground black pepper.

1   Heat the oil in a large pan. Add the onion, carrot, celery and thyme and fry gently for 20-30 minutes until soft but not brown. Add the bay leaf, chicken carcass and 900ml (1½ pints) boiling water to the pan. Bring to the boil, then reduce the heat and simmer for 5 minutes.
2   Remove the bay leaf and carcass and add the chopped roast chicken and cooked potato to the pan. Simmer for 5 minutes.
3   Whiz the soup in a food processor, pour back into the pan and bring to the boil. Stir in the cream, check the seasoning and serve immediately.

Cheap Desserts

Apple Galette

Hands-on time: 20 minutes
Cooking time: about 35 minutes

plain flour to dust

500g pack puff pastry

8 tbsp apricot jam

4 Braeburn apples, cored and very
   thinly sliced

cream or ice cream to serve (optional)

1 Preheat the oven to 200°C (180°C fan oven) mark 6. Lightly dust a worksurface with flour and roll out the pastry until it measures roughly 25.5 × 35.5cm (10 × 14in) and is 5mm (¼in) thick. Trim the edges to neaten. Put on to a large baking tray and thoroughly prick the pastry all over with a fork, leaving a 1cm (½in) border unpricked around the edge.

2 Spread half the jam over the pricked pastry, then arrange apple slices on top, overlapping them to make neat rows.

3 Bake the tart for 30–35 minutes until the pastry is golden and the apples have just started to take on colour. When the tart is 5 minutes away from the end of the cooking time, heat the remaining jam with 2 tsp water until just boiling, then carefully brush all over the apples straight after you take the tart out of the oven. Serve in slices, warm or at room temperature, with cream or ice cream, if you like.

FREEZE AHEAD

Complete the recipe, then cool the finished glazed tart and cut into slices. Wrap each slice well in non-stick baking parchment and freeze for up to 1 month (wrapped slices can be stacked on top of each other). To serve, thaw at room temperature (about 1 hour) or arrange the frozen slices on a baking tray and warm through in a preheated 150°C (130°C fan oven) mark 2 oven for 15–20 minutes until thawed.

Cuts into 8 pieces

Rhubarb and Ginger Cheesecake

Hands-on time: 25 minutes, plus chilling
Cooking time: about 2 hours, plus cooling

450g (1lb) rhubarb, cut into chunks

4 tbsp caster sugar

2 balls preserved stem ginger, syrup put to one side

175g (6oz) ginger nut biscuits, finely crushed

60g (2½oz) unsalted butter, melted

450g (1lb) cream cheese

3 medium eggs

1 tsp vanilla extract

4 tbsp icing sugar

½ tsp arrowroot

1 Put 225g (8oz) of the rhubarb chunks into a pan with the caster sugar, 3 tbsp ginger syrup and 2 tbsp cold water. Simmer for 5–10 minutes until tender. Transfer to a food processor and whiz until smooth, then leave to cool.

2 Finely chop the stem ginger and combine with the ginger nuts and butter. Press into the bottom of an 18cm (7in) round springform cake tin and chill until firm.

3 Preheat the oven to 150°C (130°C fan oven) mark 2. Whisk together the cream cheese, eggs, vanilla extract and 3 tbsp of the icing sugar. Fold in two-thirds of the rhubarb purée. Pour into the cake tin. Stir the remainder of the purée through the filling, making swirls and ripples. Bake for 1½ hours or until just set, then leave in the oven with the door ajar until cool. Chill, preferably overnight.

4 Put the remaining rhubarb into a pan with 150ml (¼ pint) cold water, the remaining icing sugar and 2 tbsp ginger syrup. Poach gently for 5–10 minutes until just tender. Remove the rhubarb and put to one side, then strain the liquid into a bowl and pour it back into the rinsed-out pan. Mix 1 tbsp of the liquid with the arrowroot until smooth, then add to the rest. Bring to the boil, then take off the heat as soon as it is slightly thickened and leave to cool.

5 To serve, remove the cheesecake from its tin and top with the poached rhubarb. Slice and drizzle with the sauce.

Cuts into 8 slices

Bread and Butter Pudding

Hands-on time: 10 minutes, plus soaking
Cooking time: about 40 minutes

50g (2oz) butter, softened, plus extra
  to grease

275g (10oz) white farmhouse bread, cut
  into 1cm (½in) slices, crusts removed

50g (2oz) raisins or sultanas

3 medium eggs

450ml (¾ pint) milk

3 tbsp golden icing sugar, plus extra
  to dust

1 Lightly grease four 300ml (½ pint)
  gratin dishes or one 1.1 litre (2 pint)
  ovenproof dish. Butter the bread, then
  cut into quarters to make triangles.
  Arrange the bread in the dish(es) and
  sprinkle with the raisins or sultanas.

2 Beat the eggs, milk and sugar in a
  bowl. Pour the mixture over the bread
  and leave to soak for 10 minutes.
  Preheat the oven to 180°C (160°C fan
  oven) mark 4.

3 Bake the pudding(s) in the oven for
  30–40 minutes. Dust with icing sugar
  to serve.

Serves 4

Freezer Feast Banoffee Cheesecake

Hands-on time: 25 minutes, plus chilling
Cooking time: about 1 hour 5 minutes, plus cooling

For the base

100g (3½oz) butter, melted, plus extra
  to grease

200g (7oz) digestive biscuits,
  finely crushed

For the filling

2 small very ripe bananas, about 150g
  (5oz) peeled weight

500g (1lb 2oz) full-fat cream cheese

200g (7oz) caster sugar

1½ tbsp plain flour

1 tsp vanilla extract

2 medium eggs, separated

To decorate

3 tbsp caramel sauce

25g (1oz) plain chocolate, shaved into
  flakes with a vegetable peeler

1 Preheat the oven to 180°C (160°C
   fan oven) mark 4. Grease a 20.5cm
   (8in) round springform tin and line
   the base with baking parchment.
   Mix together the butter and crushed
   biscuits, then press into the base of
   tin. Bake for 15 minutes, then take
   out of the oven and put to one side.
   Reduce the oven temperature to 170°C
   (150°C fan oven) mark 3.

2 To make the filling, whiz the bananas
   in a food processor until smooth.
   Add the rest of the filling ingredients
   except the egg whites to the processor
   and whiz again until smooth. Tip
   the mixture into a large bowl. In a
   separate clean bowl, whisk the egg
   whites until they hold soft peaks.
   Using a large metal spoon, fold them
   into the banana mixture.

3 Pour the mixture into the tin and
   shake gently to level. Bake for 50
   minutes or until the cheesecake is
   lightly golden – the filling will be
   wobbly, but firms up on chilling.
   Working quickly, take the cheesecake
   out of the oven and run a small knife
   around the side of the cheesecake to
   release it (this should help minimise
   cracking). Leave to cool for 30 minutes

(don't worry if a few cracks appear, they will be covered with the topping) and chill for at least 2 hours or overnight.

4 Take the cheesecake out of the tin, peel off the baking parchment and transfer to a serving plate. Allow the cheesecake to come up to room temperature (about 1 hour).

5 Put the caramel into a small bowl and whisk briefly to loosen it, then drizzle it over the top of the cheesecake. Scatter the chocolate flakes over and serve in slices.

FREEZE AHEAD
Prepare the cheesecake to the end of step 3. Wrap the cooled cheesecake (still in its tin) well with clingfilm and freeze for up to one month. To serve, allow to thaw completely in the fridge, then unwrap and complete the recipe.

Serves 8

Perfect Eggs

Eggs are a wonderfully versatile ingredient that can make a perfect pudding. All you need to remember with pancake batter is to mix quickly and lightly. For a simple yet sublime meringue, you need just egg whites and sugar. Easy!

Perfect Pancakes

To make eight pancakes, you will need:
125g (4oz) plain flour, a pinch of salt, 1 medium egg, 300ml (½ pint) milk, oil and butter to fry.

1 Sift the flour and salt into a bowl, make a well in the centre and whisk in the egg. Gradually beat in the milk to make a smooth batter, then leave to stand for 20 minutes.
2 Heat a heavy-based frying pan and coat lightly with fat. Pour in a little batter and tilt the pan to coat the bottom thinly and evenly.
3 Cook over a moderately high heat for 1 minute or until golden. Turn carefully and cook the other side for 30 seconds–1 minute.

Perfect Meringues

Baking meringues is best done whenever you know you won't be needing your oven for a good few hours, as they must be left to dry in the turned-off oven for several hours or overnight.

To make 12 meringues, you will need: 3 medium egg whites and 175g (6oz) caster sugar.

1 Preheat the oven to 170°C (150°C fan oven) mark 3. Cover a baking sheet with baking parchment.
2 Put the egg whites into a large, clean, grease-free bowl and whisk until soft peaks form. Add a spoonful of sugar and whisk until glossy.
3 Keep adding the sugar a spoonful at a time, whisking thoroughly after each addition, until you have used half the sugar. The mixture should be thick and glossy.
4 Sprinkle the remaining sugar over the mixture and then, using a metal spoon, gently fold it in.
5 Hold a dessertspoon in each hand and pick up a spoonful of mixture in one spoon, then scrape the other spoon against it to lift the mixture off. Repeat the process a few times, to form a rough oval shape. Using the empty spoon, push the oval on to the prepared baking sheet – hold it just over the sheet so that it doesn't drop from a great height. Continue this process with the remaining mixture to make 12 meringues.
6 Put the meringues into the oven and bake for 15 minutes, then turn the oven off and leave them in the oven to dry out for several hours or overnight.

3

Microwave Meringues

TAKE
5

Hands-on time: 15 minutes
Cooking time: 2 minutes

1 tbsp (15g) egg white

150g (5oz) icing sugar

250ml (9fl oz) double cream

25g (1oz) white chocolate, grated

50g (2oz) raspberries

1 Put the egg white into a large bowl, then sift in the icing sugar. Mix briefly with a wooden spoon (don't whisk), then use your hands to bring the mixture together – it will be very stiff (don't be tempted to add more egg white). Knead until smooth.

2 Divide the mixture into 16 even pieces (each should be about 10g) and roll each piece into a ball. Line the turntable in the microwave with baking parchment, then position four balls on the parchment, spacing them apart.

3 Microwave on full power (800W) for exactly 40 seconds (if your microwave is old, this can take longer). Slide the parchment and meringues out of the microwave and repeat the process with the remaining balls.

4 Whip the cream and chocolate together until the mixture just holds its shape. Briefly whip in the raspberries to create a marbling effect, then use the mixture to sandwich the meringues together. Serve.

Serves 8

Cheat's Chocolate Soufflés

Hands-on time: 15 minutes
Cooking time: about 12 minutes

butter to grease

75g (3oz) plain chocolate

225ml (8fl oz) fresh chocolate custard

3 medium egg whites

25g (1oz) caster sugar

icing sugar to dust

1 Preheat the oven to 220°C (200°C fan oven) mark 7. Put a baking sheet on the middle shelf to heat up, making sure there's enough space for the soufflés to rise. Grease six 125ml (4fl oz) ramekins.

2 Finely grate the chocolate, or whiz until it resembles breadcrumbs. Dust the insides of the ramekins with 25g (1oz) of the chocolate.

3 Mix the custard and remaining chocolate together in a large bowl. In a separate grease-free bowl, whisk the egg whites until stiff but not dry, then gradually add the caster sugar to the egg whites, whisking well after each addition. Using a metal spoon, fold the egg whites into the custard mixture.

4 Quickly divide the mixture among the prepared ramekins, put them on to the preheated baking sheet and bake for 10–12 minutes until well risen. Dust the soufflés with icing sugar and serve immediately.

Serves 6

Luscious Lemon Passion Pots

🍴 **Hands-on time:** 5 minutes, plus chilling (optional)

150g (5oz) condensed milk
50ml (2fl oz) double cream
grated zest and juice of 1 large lemon
1 passion fruit

1 Put the condensed milk, double cream and lemon zest and juice into a medium bowl and whisk until thick and fluffy. Spoon into two small ramekins or coffee cups and chill until needed – or carry on with the recipe if you can't wait.

2 To serve, halve the passion fruit, scoop out the seeds and use to decorate the lemon pots.

Serves 2

Make Your Own Ice Cream

Rich and creamy, fresh and fruity or sweet and indulgent, ice creams and iced desserts are easy to make. Good ice cream should have a smooth, creamy texture. Using an ice-cream maker is the best way to achieve it, but freezing and breaking up the ice crystals by hand works well, too.

Vanilla Ice Cream

To serve four to six, you will need: 300ml (½ pint) milk, 1 vanilla pod, split lengthways, 3 medium egg yolks, 75g (3oz) golden caster sugar, 300ml (½ pint) double cream.

1   Put the milk and vanilla pod into a pan and heat slowly until almost boiling. Take off the heat and cool for 20 minutes, then remove the vanilla pod. Whisk the egg yolks and sugar in a large bowl until thick and creamy. Gradually whisk in the milk, then strain back into the pan.

2   Cook over a low heat, stirring with a wooden spoon, until thick enough to coat the back of the spoon – do not boil. Pour into a chilled bowl and leave to cool.

3. Whisk the cream into the custard. Pour into an ice-cream maker and freeze or churn according to the manufacturer's instructions, or make by hand (see below right). Store in a covered freezerproof container for up to two months. Put the ice cream in the fridge for 15–20 minutes before serving to soften slightly.

3

SAVE EFFORT

Once you've made the custard, you can make different flavoured ice cream.

Variations

Fruit Ice Cream: sweeten 300ml (½ pint) fruit purée (such as rhubarb, gooseberry, raspberry or strawberry) to taste, then stir into the cooked custard and churn.

Chocolate Ice Cream: omit the vanilla and add 125g (4oz) plain chocolate to the milk. Heat gently until melted, then bring almost to the boil and proceed as left.

Coffee Ice Cream: omit the vanilla pod and add 150ml (¼ pint) cooled strong coffee to the cooked custard and churn.

Making ice cream by hand

1. If possible, set the freezer to fast-freeze 1 hour ahead. Pour the ice-cream mixture into a shallow freezerproof container, cover and freeze until partially frozen.
2. Spoon into a bowl and mash with a fork to break up the ice crystals. Put back into the container and freeze for 2 hours more. Repeat and freeze for a further 3 hours.

Three-ingredient Strawberry Ice Cream

🍴 **Hands-on time:** 10 minutes

500g (1lb 2oz) hulled and frozen strawberries

75g (3oz) icing sugar

125ml (4fl oz) double cream

1 Put all the ingredients into a food processor. Pulse until the strawberries are fairly broken down, then whiz until the mixture is smooth.

2 Serve immediately or transfer to a freezerproof container and freeze for up to one month. Allow to soften a little at room temperature before serving.

SAVE TIME

You can make this in advance and keep it, well wrapped, in the fridge for up to two weeks.

Serves 6

Cheat's Chocolate Fudge

TAKE
5

Hands-on time: 10 minutes
Cooking time: 2 minutes, plus chilling

500g (1lb 2oz) icing sugar

50g (2oz) cocoa powder, sifted

50ml (2fl oz) milk

50g (2oz) cold butter, chopped

a large handful of roasted and
   salted peanuts

1 Put the icing sugar and cocoa powder into a large, microwave-safe bowl and whisk to combine. Add the milk and chopped butter and microwave on full power (800W) for 2 minutes.

2 Meanwhile, line a (roughly) 15 × 25.5cm (6 × 10in) tin or serving dish with baking parchment.

3 Whisk the hot mixture until smooth (it will thicken as you do so), then stir in the nuts. Empty into the prepared tin, level the surface and chill for 20 minutes until solid. Serve in squares.

Cuts into 24 squares

Lemon Meringue Pie

Hands-on time: 30 minutes, plus chilling
Cooking time: about 1 hour, plus standing

For the pastry

225g (8oz) plain flour, plus extra to dust

a pinch of salt

150g (5oz) butter, cut into pieces

1 medium egg yolk

2 tbsp caster sugar

a little beaten egg to brush

For the filling and topping

7 medium eggs, 4 separated, at room temperature

finely grated zest of 3 lemons

175ml (6fl oz) freshly squeezed lemon juice (about 4 lemons), strained

400g can condensed milk

150ml (¼ pint) double cream

225g (8oz) golden icing sugar

SAVE EFFORT

To make a lime meringue pie, use lime zest and juice instead of lemon.

1 Sift the flour and salt into a clean mound on a clean surface. Make a large well in the centre and add the butter, egg yolk, sugar and 3 tbsp cold water. Using the fingertips of one hand, work the butter, egg yolk, sugar and water together until well blended. Gradually work in all the flour to bind the mixture together. Knead the dough gently on a lightly floured surface until smooth, then wrap in clingfilm and leave to rest in the fridge for at least 30 minutes before rolling out.

2 Roll out the pastry on a lightly floured surface and use to line a 23cm (9in), 4cm (1½in) deep, loose-based fluted tart tin. Prick the base with a fork and chill for 30 minutes. Meanwhile, preheat the oven to 190°C (170°C fan oven) mark 5.

3 Bake the pastry case blind for 10 minutes at each stage. Brush the inside with beaten egg and put back into the oven for 1 minute to seal.

Increase the oven temperature to 180°C (160°C fan oven) mark 4.

4 To make the filling, put 4 egg yolks into a bowl with the 3 whole eggs. Add the lemon zest and juice and whisk lightly. Stir in the condensed milk and cream.

5 Pour the filling into the pastry case and bake for 30 minutes or until just set in the centre. Leave to cool while you prepare the meringue. Increase the oven temperature to 200°C (180°C fan oven) mark 6.

6 For the meringue, using a hand-held electric whisk, whisk the egg whites and icing sugar together in a heatproof bowl over a pan of gently simmering water for 10 minutes or until shiny and thick. Take off the heat and continue to whisk at low speed for 5–10 minutes until the bowl is cool. Pile the meringue on to the filling and swirl to form peaks. Bake for 5–10 minutes until the meringue is tinged brown. Leave to stand for about 1 hour, then serve.

Serves 8

Calorie Gallery

453 cal ♥ 22g protein
25g fat (6g sat) ♥ 3g fibre
38g carb ♥ 1.6g salt

12

389 cal ♥ 17g protein
18g fat (10g sat) ♥ 2g fibre
41g carb ♥ 2.8g salt

14

432 cal ♥ 20g protein
20g fat (7g sat) ♥ 5g fibre
46g carb ♥ 1.8g salt

18

121 cal ♥ 5g protein
6g fat (1g sat) ♥ 2g fibre
11g carb ♥ 0.9g salt

20

223 cal ♥ 9g protein
10g fat (2g sat) ♥ 1g fibre
22g carb ♥ 1.4g salt

34

339 cal ♥ 26g protein
11g fat (2g sat) ♥ 3g fibre
37g carb ♥ 0.4g salt

36

240 cal ♥ 15g protein
9g fat (2g sat) ♥ 3g fibre
25g carb ♥ 1.6g salt

38

517 cal ♥ 34g protein
21g fat (8g sat) ♥ 6g fibre
51g carb ♥ 0.8g salt

52

654 cal ♥ 12g protein
35g fat (18g sat) ♥ 5g fibre
67g carb ♥ 3.3g salt

56

313 cal ♥ 22g protein
16g fat (4g sat) ♥ 7g fibre
24g carb ♥ 1.8g salt

58

513 cal ♥ 35g protein
19g fat (7g sat) ♥ 5g fibre
54g carb ♥ 1.1g salt

70

324 cal ♥ 26g protein
15g fat (4g sat) ♥ 2g fibre
24g carb ♥ 1.3g salt

72

349 cal ♥ 20g protein
16g fat (5g sat) ♥ 10g fibre
34g carb ♥ 3.3g salt

74

519 cal ♥ 33g protein
14g fat (4g sat) ♥ 3g fibre
65g carb ♥ 1.3g salt

76

506 cal ♥ 10g protein
3g fat (5g sat) ♥ 4g fibre
46g carb ♥ 1.2g salt

197 cal ♥ 4g protein
8g fat (1g sat) ♥ 3g fibre
29g carb ♥ 1.3g salt

26

76 cal ♥ 2g protein
3g fat (0.5g sat) ♥ 2g fibre
11g carb ♥ 0.1g salt

28

261 cal ♥ 23g protein
16g fat (10g sat) ♥ 1g fibre
9g carb ♥ 2.3g salt

32

474 cal ♥ 8g protein
15g fat (4g sat) ♥ 4g fibre
79g carb ♥ 1.3g salt

566 cal ♥ 35g protein
30g fat (5g sat) ♥ 3g fibre
40g carb ♥ 0.9g salt

46

485 cal ♥ 12g protein
33g fat (17g sat) ♥ 1g fibre
27g carb ♥ 1.5g salt

48

478 cal ♥ 30g protein
26g fat (9g sat) ♥ 0.6g fibre
19g carb ♥ 2.8g salt

50

398 cal ♥ 25g protein
g fat (9g sat) ♥ 1g fibre
21g carb ♥ 1.1g salt

591 cal ♥ 39g protein
31g fat (17g sat) ♥ 4g fibre
41g carb ♥ 1.3g salt

62

461 cal ♥ 37g protein
28g fat (11g sat) ♥ 0.4g fibre
10g carb ♥ 1.2g salt

64

532 cal ♥ 25g protein
19g fat (9g sat) ♥ 4g fibre
71g carb ♥ 1.8g salt

68

220 cal ♥ 23g protein
g fat (3g sat) ♥ 2g fibre
8g carb ♥ 0.7g salt

421 cal ♥ 40g protein
25g fat (14g sat) ♥ 0.9g fibre
6g carb ♥ 1.0g salt

82

475 cal ♥ 17g protein
9g fat (1g sat) ♥ 6g fibre
87g carb ♥ 1.6g salt

84

933 cal ♥ 23g protein
71g fat (32g sat) ♥ 3g fibre
56g carb ♥ 2.5g salt

86

390 cal ♥ 35g protein
28g fat (11g sat) ♥ 0.5g fibre
1g carb ♥ 2.4g salt

88

703 cal ♥ 27g protein
24g fat (14g sat) ♥ 4g fibre
102g carb ♥ 1.3g salt

96

582 cal ♥ 19g protein
23g fat (12g sat) ♥ 4g fibre
76g carb ♥ 0.9g salt

98

587 cal ♥ 40g protein
17g fat (3g sat) ♥ 9g fibre
76g carb ♥ 1.3g salt

100

282 cal ♥ 21g protein
15g fat (3g sat) ♥ 3g fibre
16g carb ♥ 1.9g salt

112

437 cal ♥ 18g protein
28g fat (15g sat) ♥ 7g fibre
31g carb ♥ 1.7g salt

114

480 cal ♥ 50g protein
17g fat (7g sat) ♥ 1g fibre
48g carb ♥ 1.8g salt

116

254 cal ♥ 27g protein
6g fat (1g sat) ♥ 2g fibre
27g carb ♥ 0.9g salt

118

372 cal ♥ 27g protein
12g fat (4g sat) ♥ 2g fibre
42g carb ♥ 2.2g salt

132

591 cal ♥ 26g protein
34g fat (16g sat) ♥ 1g fibre
42g carb ♥ 1.5g salt

136

539 cal ♥ 36g protein
19g fat (5g sat) ♥ 12g fibre
58g carb ♥ 2.5g salt

138

447 cal ♥ 18g protein
7g fat (3g sat) ♥ 4g fib
82g carb ♥ 1.9g salt

140

247 cal ♥ 1g protein
18g fat (11g sat) ♥ 0.2g fibre
22g carb ♥ 0g salt

156

126 cal ♥ 3g protein
5g fat (2g sat) ♥ 0.4g fibre
19g carb ♥ 0.1g salt

158

377 cal ♥ 7g protein
21g fat (13g sat) ♥ 0.3g fibre
43g carb ♥ 0.3g salt

160

175 cal ♥ 1g protein
11g fat (7g sat) ♥ 0.9g fibre
18g carb ♥ 0g salt

164

598 cal ♥ 33g protein
5g fat (9g sat)♥ 3g fibre
65g carb ♥ 2.2g salt

650 cal ♥ 40g protein
33g fat (15g sat)♥ 4g fibre
55g carb ♥ 2.2g salt
106

544 cal ♥ 29g protein
39g fat (18g sat) ♥ 0.4g fibre
21g carb ♥ 1.1g salt
108

411 cal ♥ 26g protein
24g fat (7g sat) ♥ 0.7g fibre
24g carb ♥ 0.7g salt
110

327 cal ♥ 19g protein
6g fat (6g sat) ♥ 0g fibre
1g carb ♥ 0.1g salt

425 cal ♥ 21g protein
6g fat (1g sat) ♥ 2g fibre
67g carb ♥ 0.9g salt
122

373 cal ♥ 23g protein
22g fat (4g sat) ♥ 2g fibre
23g carb ♥ 2.0g salt
128

427 cal ♥ 18g protein
9g fat (2g sat) ♥ 4g fibre
72g carb ♥ 1.6g salt
130

344 cal ♥ 4g protein
g fat (10g sat) ♥ 0.9g fibre
45g carb ♥ 0.5g salt

530 cal ♥ 6g protein
39g fat (23g sat) ♥ 1g fibre
40g carb ♥ 0.9g salt
148

450 cal ♥ 16g protein
13g fat (5g sat) ♥ 1g fibre
70g carb ♥ 1.1g salt
150

691 cal ♥ 6g protein
50g fat (29g sat) ♥ 0.8g fibre
57g carb ♥ 0.9g salt
152

111 cal ♥ 1g protein
fat (2g sat) ♥ 0.4g fibre
22g carb ♥ 0.1g salt

692 cal ♥ 14g protein
36g fat (21g sat) ♥ 0.9g fibre
83g carb ♥ 0.6g salt
168

Index

PICTURE CREDITS

Photographers: Steve Baxter (pages 15, 19, 25, 27, 33, 35, 97, 99, 101, 105, 107, 109, 111, 113, 115, 117, 119, 121, 123, 129, 131, 133, 137, 139 and 141); Martin Brigdale (page 37); Nicki Dowey (page 39); Gareth Morgans (pages 45, 47, 49, 51, 53, 57, 59, 61, 63, 65, 69, 71, 73, 75, 77, 81, 83, 85, 87, 89, 147, 153, 159, 161 and 165); Myles New (pages 157 and 167); Craig Robertson (pages 16, 151, 154, 155, 162, 163 and 169); Lucinda Symons (page 13); Philip Webb (pages 21, 29 and 149).

Home Economists:
Joanna Farrow, Emma Jane Frost, Teresa Goldfinch, Alice Hart, Lucy McKelvie, Kim Morphew, Aya Nishimura, Bridget Sargeson, Kate Trend and Mari Mereid Williams.

Stylists:
Tamzin Ferdinando, Wei Tang, Helen Trent and Fanny Ward.

BAKE ME A CAKE

There's always time for cake

EASY PEASY MEALS

Easy meals for every day

LET'S DO BRUNCH

Mouth-watering meals to start your day

CHEAP EATS

Budget-busting ideas that won't break the bank

SALAD DAYS

Oh-so-fresh ideas for fabulous salads

Available online at store.anovabooks.com and from all good bookshops

POSH NOSH

Delicious recipes to impress your guests

PARTY FOOD

Delicious recipes to get the party started

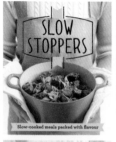

SLOW STOPPERS

Slow-cooked meals packed with flavour

GREAT VEG

Inspired ideas for delicious veggie meals

AL FRESCO EATS

Easy grills, barbecues and picnics

ROAST IT

There's nothing better than a delicious roast

FLASH IN THE PAN

Spice up your noodles and stir-fries

GLUTEN-FREE AND EASY

Oh-so-good-for-you recipes that taste great

LOW FAT LOW CAL

Nice recipes don't need to be naughty